# Foul Facts from the Perilous Past

# Foul Facts from the Perilous Past

By Tracey Turner

Pictures by Sally Kindberg

ENGLISH HERITAGE

Published by English Heritage, Isambard House, Kemble Drive,
Swindon SN2 2GZ
www.english-heritage.org.uk

English Heritage is the Government's statutory advisor on all aspects
of the historic environment.

First published 2007

10 9 8 7 6 5 4 3 2 1

ISBN-13 978 185074 992 9

Product code 51138

*British Library Cataloguing in Publication data*
A CIP catalogue for this book is available from the British Library.

Edited and brought to publication by René Rodgers,
English Heritage Publishing
Design by René Rodgers, English Heritage Publishing
Design consultant: Neil Collins, English Heritage Creative Services
Printed in the United Kingdom by Cambridge University Press

# Contents

# DATE LIST

The foul facts in this book aren't in date order – these lists show when many of the historical figures in this book lived, ruled and died, so you'll know when all the gruesome stuff happened.

Here are the emperors, kings, queens and other rulers that are mentioned in this book for doing something foul.

- Boudicca – died AD 60/61
- Julius Caesar – 100–44 BC; ruled 49–44 BC
- Emperor Caligula – AD 12–41; ruled AD 37–41
- Emperor Claudius – 10 BC–AD 54; ruled AD 41–54
- Emperor Nero – AD 37–68; ruled AD 54–68
- Emperor Domitian – AD 51–96; ruled AD 81–96
- Emperor Commodus – AD 161–192; ruled AD 180–192
- Emperor Septimius Severus – AD 146–211; ruled AD 193–211
- Emperor Elagabalus – c AD 203–222; ruled AD 218–222
- Emperor Valerian – c AD 200–260; ruled AD 253–260
- Oswald of Northumbria (later St Oswald) – c 604–642; ruled 634–642
- Penda of Mercia – died 655; ruled 626–655
- Ragnar Hairy-Breeches – died 865
- King Aella of Northumberland – died 867; ruled c 862–867
- King Edmund of East Anglia – c 840–870; ruled 855–870
- Charles the Simple of France – 879–929; ruled 893–922/923

- King Ethelred II – 968–1016; ruled 978–1016
- King Harold – c 1022–1066; ruled 1066
- William the Conqueror – c 1028–1087; ruled 1066–1087
- William II (William Rufus) – c 1056–1100; ruled 1087–1100
- Henry I – c 1068–1135; ruled 1100–1135
- King Stephen – c 1096–1154; ruled 1135–1154
- Matilda (known as Empress Matilda) – 1101–1167
- Henry II – 1133–1189; ruled 1154–1189
- Richard I – 1157–1199; ruled 1189–1199
- King John – c 1167–1216; ruled 1199–1216
- Henry III – 1207–1272; ruled 1216–1272
- Edward I – 1239–1307; ruled 1272–1307
- Edward II – 1284–1327; ruled 1307–1327
- Edward III – 1312–1377; ruled 1327–1377
- Richard II – 1367–1400; ruled 1377–1399
- Henry IV – 1367–1413; ruled 1399–1413
- Henry V – 1387–1422; ruled 1413–1422
- Edward IV – 1442–1483; ruled 1461–1470 and 1471–1483
- Edward V – 1470–1483?; ruled 1483
- Richard III – 1452–1485; ruled 1483–1485
- Henry VII (Henry Tudor) – 1457–1509; ruled 1485–1509
- Henry VIII – 1491–1547; ruled 1509–1547
- Edward VI – 1537–1553; ruled 1547–1553
- Lady Jane Grey – c 1537–1554; ruled 9 days in July 1553
- Mary Tudor – 1516–1558; ruled 1553–1558
- Elizabeth I – 1533–1603; ruled 1558–1603
- Mary Queen of Scots – 1542–1587; ruled 1542–1567
- James I – 1566–1625; ruled Scotland 1567–1625, ruled England and Ireland 1603–1625
- Charles I – 1600–1649; ruled 1625–1649

- Oliver Cromwell – 1599-1658; ruled 1653-1658
- Charles II – 1630-1685; ruled 1660-1685
- James II of England – 1633-1701; ruled 1685-1688
- William III – 1650-1702; ruled 1689-1702
- Queen Anne – 1665-1714; ruled 1702-1714
- George I – 1660-1727; ruled 1714-1727
- George II – 1683-1760; ruled 1727-1760
- George III – 1738-1820; ruled 1760-1820
- Louis XVI of France – 1754-1793; ruled 1774-1792
- George IV – 1762-1830; ruled 1820-1830
- Queen Victoria – 1819-1901; ruled 1837-1901
- Edward VII – 1841-1910; ruled 1901-1910

These people also have something unpleasant about them.
- Spartacus – c 120-70 BC
- Saints Andronicus, Probus and Tarachus – died c AD 304
- Rollo the Viking – c 860-932
- William Iron Arm – before 1010-1046
- Harald Hardrada – 1015-1066
- Odo, Bishop of Bayeux – c 1036-1097
- Herward the Wake – he was most foul between 1070-1071
- William Aetheling – 1103-1120
- Thomas Becket – c 1118-1170
- Countess of Buchan – c 1270-after 1313
- William Wallace – c 1270-1305
- Geoffrey Chaucer – c 1343-1400
- Sir Thomas More – 1478-1535
- Anne Boleyn – c 1500-1536
- George Gordon, Earl of Huntly – 1513-1562

- Anne of Cleves – 1515–1557
- Catherine Parr – c 1512–1548
- Sir Walter Raleigh – c 1552–1618
- William Shakespeare – 1564–1616
- Guy Fawkes – 1570–1606
- Sir Arthur Aston – 1590–1649
- Samuel Pepys – 1633–1703
- Isaac Newton – 1643–1727
- Judge George Jeffreys – 1645–1689
- Matthew Hopkins – died 1647
- Duke of Monmouth – 1649–1685
- Edward Teach (Blackbeard) – c 1675–1718
- John Hunter – 1728–1793
- Captain James Cook – 1728–1779
- Captain Robert Jenkins – he was most foul in 1731–1745
- Admiral Horatio Nelson – 1758–1805
- Sir Henry Halford – 1766–1844
- Charles Darwin – 1809–1882
- Karl Marx – 1818–1883
- Prince Albert – 1819–1861
- Reverend Thomas Baker – died 1867
- Prince Christian – 1831–1917
- Harold Davidson – 1875–1937
- Albert Einstein – 1879–1955
- Vladimir Lenin – 1870–1924
- Emily Davison – 1872–1913
- Marie Curie – 1867–1934
- Captain Robert Falcon Scott – 1868–1912
- Adolf Hitler – 1889–1945
- Heinrich Himmler – 1900–1945

# The Prehistoric Perilous Past

🐞 The Romans said that the Celts built huge models of men out of wicker, then filled the wicker men with human sacrifice victims and set fire to them. No one knows whether or not it's really true.

🐞 Jewellery was as popular in prehistory as it is today, just a bit more ghastly: people made jewellery from animal teeth and claws and even the bodies of insects.

🐞 In ancient Jericho, in what's now the Middle East, people kept the skulls of their dead relatives. They covered them with plaster to recreate the dead person's face and popped on a couple of shells for eyes. The skulls were kept in pride of place in people's living rooms.

🐞 Woodhenge is an ancient site near Stonehenge in Wiltshire. Right in the middle of it, the skeleton of a three-year-old child has been found – the skull was split with an axe. This is thought to be evidence of a human sacrifice from the time when Woodhenge was first built.

# GORY STORY: A BODY IN THE BOG

In 1984 a workman cutting peat in Lindow Moss, Cheshire, got a nasty surprise. He found a dead body in the bog, the grisly remains of a 2,000-year-old murder victim. Only half the body remained (the rest of it had been destroyed by machinery), but from it experts could piece together an ancient mystery. During the Iron Age, a fit young man had been whacked on the back of the head, strangled and then had his throat cut. Finally he was thrown naked into the bog. The man's last meal was discovered in his stomach: a cake made from wheat, rye and barley. Some people think that the man was a Druid (a Celtic priest) who had eaten his last ritual meal, then been sacrificed by other Druids.

🐞 Boudicca was a Celtic queen who led a rebellion against the Romans. When she was defeated, it was said that she killed herself by drinking poison.

# BELIEVE IT OR NOT?

**The first brain surgeons lived in the Stone Age.**
Believe it or not, it's true. We know that ancient people
had holes made in their heads because lots of ancient
skulls have been found with holes cut into them. An
ancient surgeon would use a flint knife to cut into the
patient's scalp, peel back the skin and then
make a hole in the skull. One skull was
found with a hole measuring more than 50
square centimetres! The earliest
example was a skull with
two holes in it that was
found in France – it dates
from 7,000 years ago.

🐞 Celtic priests, the
Druids, supposedly made
sacrifices of animals and
humans to their gods.

🐞 Animal stomachs made good (but gruesome) bags and
cooking pots in the Stone Age.

🐞 Druids believed that eating the flesh of dogs, cats and
bulls would reveal the animals' secrets to them.

🐞 Stone Age people used moss, leaves, stones and clumps
of grass as loo paper.

🐞 Celtic warriors collected heads from their fallen enemies and would remove their brains and mix them with lime to make a hard, round ball as a gruesome war trophy.

🐞 In 1991, a 5,000-year-old mummified body was found preserved in the ice in the Alps mountains on the border between Italy and Austria. The body is of a 40-year-old man and it's the oldest frozen mummy ever found. Some people think that he was the victim of a Stone Age crime: there was an arrowhead embedded in his shoulder.

🐞 A graveyard has been uncovered from about 2,500 years ago in modern-day Israel. But people aren't buried there: it's a graveyard for dogs. Each one of the 700 or so animals has been carefully buried in exactly the same position.

🐞 In the Stone Age, the women of one village in Italy had some of their front teeth pulled out. The archaeologists who discovered their skeletons believe the women might have had the teeth removed because they thought it made them more beautiful. Sounds strange – but is it any stranger than having your tongue pierced?

🐞 The stone circle at Avebury in Wiltshire is much bigger than the one found at Stonehenge, but over the years people have removed several of the stones. In the Middle Ages, a travelling barber was helping to knock down one of the stones and it fell on top of him. His squished skeleton was discovered in the 1930s.

🐞 Celtic warriors fought with swords and spears, and the Romans claimed that they sometimes went into battle with absolutely no clothes on. Perhaps the Celts thought it would frighten their enemies.

🐞 There were slaves in Celtic times – one Roman writer mentions that the Romans sent slaves from Britain to Rome during the Iron Age.

🐞 Horrible-looking iron neck shackles have been found in north Wales dating from the Iron Age. They could have been used to join together five prisoners, slaves or even sacrifice victims.

🐞 The Celts believed that an enemy could still harm you even after he was dead, unless you chopped his head off.

🐛 Archaeologists have studied human poo from thousands of years ago and discovered something foul: in some parts of the world, ancient people ate human brains (and other bits of people too).

🐛 If you lived in prehistoric times you'd probably have eaten animals' innards, eyeballs, noses and other squishy and gristly bits, as well as the flesh. Insects, grubs and other creepy crawlies were also a good source of protein.

# BELIEVE IT OR NOT?

**People had tattoos in the Stone Age.**
Believe it or not, it's true. The body of the Stone Age man preserved in the ice in the Alps has 57 tattoos on it. The tattoos are on the parts of the body where the man had inflamed joints, so they might have been an attempt to make him better.

🐛 Every New Year the Celts killed tiny birds called wrens. They believed it brought good luck (though not to the wrens, obviously).

🐛 Celts sometimes exiled criminals by casting them adrift in an open boat without a paddle. If they drifted back to shore, they'd be enslaved.

# GORY STORY: HORRIBLE CELTIC HEADHUNTERS

A Roman writer said that after the Celts cut off their dead enemies' heads, they hung them from the necks of their horses as they charged into battle. Historians thought that he might have been making the Celts sound more horrible than they really were, until a gruesome burial site was uncovered...

In France during the First World War soldiers were digging a trench when they discovered evidence of a prehistoric battle: the bones of about 500 Celtic warriors. The most surprising thing about the skeletons was that all the skulls had been removed – the heads had been sliced off with knives.

🐞 Some Stone Age dead bodies were left out for birds to pick clean of flesh, so that just the bones remained. Eventually, the bones were buried.

🐞 Celtic men went into battle with their hair sticking up in spikes – they used lime to harden and bleach it.

🐞 Celtic kings were buried with all sorts of things, such as chariots, weapons, jewellery, wine and cups. One king was even buried with his toenail clippers!

# BELIEVE IT OR NOT?

**Prehistoric people ate food from animals' stomachs.**
Believe it or not, it's true. When they'd killed an animal, prehistoric people would sometimes open its stomach to see if it contained anything nice and fresh for them to eat. This could be especially useful when fresh greens were in short supply in the winter time. The next time you're told to eat up your vegetables, be grateful you didn't live thousands of years ago.

🐞 Archaeologists have found evidence of a massacre that happened about 14,000 years ago in the area that's now Egypt. Skeletons of 58 people, including young children, were found: some of them had the arrowheads that killed them still stuck in their bones.

🐞 At the festival of Samhain, the Celts believed that the dead could return to haunt the places they had lived. We have a spooky celebration at the same time of year: we call it Halloween.

🐞 Celtic warriors believed that keeping an enemy's severed head would give them that enemy's wisdom and power. They preserved their favourite heads in oil.

🐞 At least one poor Stone Age person was killed by an arrow up his nose! A skull has been found with an arrowhead still embedded in it, showing that the arrow must have entered through the nostril. That must have really hurt!

🐞 Some people claim that Celtic Queen Boudicca is buried underneath Platform 10 of King's Cross Station in London.

🐞 The Celts held the strange belief that if you were wounded, a dog's lick would help to heal it. (Do NOT try this at home!)

# PREHISTORIC QUIZ

🐞 Not all of the answers to the quizzes can be found in the text – you might need to look up some foul facts on your own!

1. What was Ogham?

a) An ancient sacrifice
b) Stone Age food made from intestines
c) The written language of the Celts

2. Bone, tusks and teeth were all used as what in the Stone Age?

a) Jewellery
b) Toothpicks
c) Money

3. Which of the following poisonous plants is associated with the Druids?

a) Deadly nightshade
b) Mistletoe
c) Foxglove

4. Which of the following was found in ancient holes surrounding Stonehenge?

a) The remains of sacrificed animals
b) Ancient poo
c) Burnt human bodies

5. The Celts believed that their war-goddesses appeared on battlefields disguised as which of the following animals?

a) Dogs
b) Rats
c) Crows

6. Which of the following did the Celts wear that people still wear today?

a) Eyeshadow
b) Top hats
c) Nose studs

7. What did the colour red mean to the Celts?

a) Death
b) Danger
c) Good luck

8. What was found in the Alps and is known as Otzi?

a) A Bronze Age treasure chest
b) A Stone Age mummy
c) The skeleton of an Iron Age man

9. How do we think ancient people transported the great stones to Stonehenge?

a) They were pulled by oxen on carts.
b) They were pulled along on rollers.
c) They were loaded on to woolly mammoths.

10. What happened when the Celtic King Prasutagus died?

a) His son defeated the Romans.
b) His wife led a rebellion against the Romans.
c) A Roman was made king of Prasutagus's tribe.

# The Roman Perilous Past

🐞 The Romans left large containers in the street to collect the pee of passers-by: they used it to clean laundry.

🐞 Life was tough for cockerels and rams in ancient Rome. They were thought to be holy animals and were often used as victims of sacrifice. Priests would foretell the future by looking at their splattered insides.

🐞 A Roman cure for toothache was strapping a toad to the jaw.

🐞 Ancient Romans used sponges on sticks instead of loo paper. After the sponge had been used it was rinsed in running water and left for the next person.

🐞 The Romans punished some criminals by throwing them unarmed to wild animals in the arena, a punishment that was considered disgraceful. Upper-class citizens who were given the death penalty were usually beheaded.

Roman food included snails fattened on milk until they couldn't get back into their shells, peacock tongues, chickens that had been drowned in red wine and dormice fed on nuts.

# BELIEVE IT OR NOT?

**Roman plays had real murders in them.**
Believe it or not, it's true. The Romans were a really bloodthirsty lot. Their Games were especially gruesome, but even a trip to the theatre called for a strong stomach. If someone was killed in the plot of a play, sometimes a condemned criminal was brought in and actually killed on stage. Some cruel playwrights made up plots with the most horrific murders in them just so that the audience would be treated to an especially gory spectacle.

If a Roman slave gave evidence in a law court, the evidence was only valid if the slave had been tortured first!

Julius Caesar was captured by pirates when he was a young man. He became quite friendly with the pirates and, when he managed to raise money for his ransom, the pirates set him free. Then Caesar hunted down the pirates and had them all executed.

# GORY STORY: NERO'S MUM

The Emperor Nero wasn't famous for his kindness, and his mother, Agrippina the Younger, was a bit of a horror too. Agrippina plotted against her own brother, the ghastly Emperor Caligula, and had to stay away from Rome until after he died. She killed her second husband to get at his money, then married her uncle, the Emperor Claudius. Having made sure that he had adopted her son, Nero, she poisoned Claudius.

Nero became emperor after Claudius, as Agrippina had planned, but he wasn't very grateful to his mother. He tried to kill Agrippina several times: a few times with poison and once by sinking her boat in the Bay of Naples (she managed to swim ashore). He even tried to kill her by collapsing a ceiling on top of her bed! Finally Nero sent assassins to murder his mother at her country house and they succeeded.

Roman soldiers had to stay in the army for at least 25 years and weren't allowed to get married until they left.

It was fashionable for Roman women to have pale skin, so they used make-up made from white lead. Lead is poisonous and very bad for the skin, unfortunately, so the more women used the make-up, the worse their skin looked underneath it. Eventually the lead in the make-up could kill the women who wore it.

The most terrible Roman punishment was reserved for someone who killed his or her own father. They would be beaten, then made to get into a sack with a snake, a dog, a monkey and a rooster; the sack was then sewn up and thrown into the River Tiber.

Wild beasts were brought from different parts of the Roman Empire to take part in the ghastly Games in Rome. Armed men called gladiators fought against animals (and each other too) and animals were also made to fight against one another. Elephants against bulls featured in the Games in 79 BC.

Roman ladies used black hair dye that was made from leeches.

🐞 After hundreds of plague-free years, there were two outbreaks of plague in Rome. During the second outbreak, in AD 179, the disease killed around 2,000 people every day. This was not the last time the plague came to Rome – it returned many more times afterwards.

🐞 The Emperor Valerian was captured by the Persian ruler Shapur, who killed him. The story goes that Shapur had Valerian's body stuffed and put on display as a gruesome trophy.

🐞 Roman toothpaste contained ground-up dogs' teeth, ash, oyster shells and honey.

🐞 Emperor Claudius made a law that allowed people to fart at the dinner table.

🐞 Public loos in the Roman Empire were very public – everybody sat or stood in the same multi-seated toilet, then used the communal sponges on sticks afterwards. Some public toilets could seat up to 100 people.

# GORY STORY: ANDRONICUS, PROBUS AND TARACHUS

Christians provided the bloodthirsty Romans with more people to kill for their entertainment. Nero started it: he accused Christians of starting a great fire in Rome and put many of them to death. Throwing unarmed Christians to hungry lions was a popular method of execution. Many of the executed Christians were later made into saints and many of them have gory stories. For example, Saints Andronicus, Probus and Tarachus were three Christian men executed during the reign of Diocletian. They were beaten with stones, burned, whipped and stabbed, and *then* they were thrown to wild animals. The story goes that the animals refused to touch the men (because they were so holy), so the Romans had to chop their heads off instead. How disappointing for them.

About 60 members of the Roman Senate (a bit like today's MPs) plotted against Julius Caesar and assassinated him in 44 BC. They hid knives beneath their togas, then attacked him as he arrived to start the day's business. He was stabbed more than 20 times.

After an argument with Julius Caesar, Roman general Pompey ran away to Egypt and was then murdered. His head was cut off and given to Caesar in a basket as a thoughtful gift.

In the famous Roman baths, people would clean themselves by getting hot and sweaty, then scraping the dirt off with a special scraper called a *strigil*.

Escaped gladiator Spartacus led 70,000 rebel slaves to victory against two Roman legions. The rebels were finally defeated and 6,000 of them were crucified (hanged on crosses until they were dead) beside the road into Rome.

# BELIEVE IT OR NOT?

**One Roman emperor fought as a gladiator.**
Believe it or not, it's true. Emperor Commodus is said to have fought as a gladiator during his reign. He won no fewer than 735 times – his opponents were given weapons made of lead, so Commodus had a bit of an unfair advantage. He paid himself a massive wad of money for his gladiatorial matches, which was generous of him. Commodus wasn't very popular and eventually he was murdered - an assassin strangled him while he was sleeping in his bed.

In AD 64 a big section of the city of Rome burned down. People blamed Emperor Nero (they thought he did it to make room for new buildings for himself). However, he blamed the Christians – and had lots of them executed.

The Emperor Nero accused his first wife, Claudia Octavia, of having other boyfriends and eventually he sentenced her to death. His second wife, Poppaea Sabina, didn't last very long either: Nero is supposed to have kicked her to death when she complained that he'd come home late.

Emperor Elagabalus was murdered by his own bodyguards, stuffed into a sewer and then thrown into the River Tiber.

Newborn babies were laid at the feet of their fathers during the Roman period. If the Roman dad picked up his baby, it would live. But if he ignored it, the baby would be taken away and left to die.

During the Roman period, women also fought in the arena as gladiators. Emperor Domitian liked to watch gladiatorial fights between dwarfs and women. However, Emperor Septimius Severus banned women from fighting in AD 200.

# BELIEVE IT OR NOT?

**The Romans had a goddess of sewers.**
Believe it or not, it's true. Venus Cloacina was the goddess of Rome's main sewer system and her shrine was also the entrance to the sewer.

🐞 Emperor Caligula drank pearls dissolved in vinegar, ordered his army to collect seashells, and tried to make his favourite horse a politician. He was cruel as well as crazy: he had rich people murdered to get their money and it was said that he condemned criminals to death so that there was a good supply of victims to be thrown to wild animals in the bloodthirsty Roman Games.

🐞 In a Roman household, the father had the power of life and death over his family and slaves. He could have any one of them executed if he thought they deserved it.

🐞 During the Games held in honour of Julius Caesar's daughter's funeral, no fewer than 300 pairs of gladiators fought against one another.

🐞 There was a rebellion against Emperor Nero and he was sentenced to be flogged to death, but he killed himself with a dagger before the sentence could be carried out.

🐞 Emperor Claudius was poisoned by his own wife with a dish of mushrooms.

# ROMAN QUIZ

1. What was a *subligaculum*?

a) A pair of Roman pants
b) A Roman public toilet
c) A type of gladiator

2. Which of these was supposed to cure epilepsy?

a) The blood of a dead cockerel
b) The blood of a dead priestess
c) The blood of a dead gladiator

3. How was the Roman sauce *liquamen* made?

a) From mashed-up sheeps' eyeballs
b) From snails fed on red wine and liquidised
c) From ground-up fish that was left in the sun to ferment

4. Which weapons were carried by a gladiator known as a *retiarius*?

a) A net, a trident and a dagger
b) A sword, a shield and a spear
c) A catapult, an axe and a club

5. The emperor Caligula is supposed to have planned to make his favourite horse ...?

a) A gold toga
b) A god
c) A politician

6. According to Roman legend, who looked after Romulus and Remus, the founders of Rome, when they were children?

a) A bear
b) A wolf
c) A hippopotamus

7. How many animals were killed for the opening of the Colosseum in Rome (the site where the Games were held) in AD 80?

a) 900
b) 9,000
c) 90,000

8. According to an ancient historian, Emperor Elagabalus ate which of the following?

a) Camels' heels, flamingos' brains and cocks' combs
b) Pigs' trotters, ducks' bills and porcupine quills
c) Rhino horns, elephants' trunks and bears' paws

9. What did the Romans use to bleach their hair?

a) Crushed beetles
b) Pigeon poo
c) Dog poo

10. True or false? Roman doctors performed plastic surgery.

# The Saxon & Viking Perilous Past

🐛 Saxons were sometimes known to skin their dead Viking enemies and hang the skins on church doors.

🐛 The Saxons thought illness was caused by elves. If your horse was sick, you could make a hole in its ear and then give the horse a good beating to drive the elves out.

🐛 Saxon monks wrote on sheets called vellum made out of the dried stomachs of calves.

🐛 Vikings had some foul-sounding nicknames: Ragnar Hairy-Breeches, Einar Belly-Shaker and Ulf the Unwashed.

🐞 When he was a baby, Saxon King Ethelred II peed into the baptismal font at his christening. It was taken to be a very bad omen (and he did end up being a bit of a useless king – he even became known as Ethelred the Unready).

🐞 The Saxons didn't have prisons and people were often punished with fines. For some crimes, a body part might be cut off.

🐞 If you caught a beetle and threw it over your left shoulder, it was supposed to cure a Saxon stomach-ache.

🐞 If a Viking died away from his homeland, his friends would put the body in a pot to boil the

ache

flesh from the bones. Then the bones could be easily carried back home.

🐞 The Saxons sometimes buried servants with their masters. But they didn't bother to make sure they were dead first – they buried them alive!

🐞 The crime of making fake coins had a very nasty punishment in Saxon times: the criminal's hands were cut off and nailed to the door of the building where the coins had been made.

# BELIEVE IT OR NOT?

**A Saxon's nose was worth twice his ear.**
Believe it or not, it's true. If you killed or injured
someone, you had to pay a certain price to their family.
The price depended on how important the person was, or
which body part you'd injured. If you killed a peasant, for
example, you'd have to pay his family 200 shillings. If you
just chopped off his ear, you'd only owe him 30 shillings.
But a nose would cost you twice that amount.

Saxons who ran away from their punishment were
declared 'outlaws'. No one would be punished for doing
harm to an outlaw.

Both Saxons and Vikings loved feasting and drinking.
They often drank far too much – this wasn't helped by the
fact that drinking cups were shaped so that you couldn't
put them down unless they were empty.

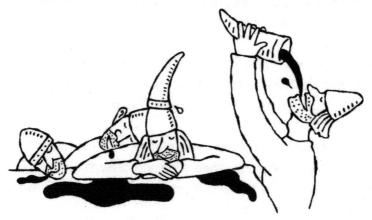

🐞 The Saxon king, Aella of Northumberland, captured and killed the Viking leader, Ragnar Hairy-Breeches. The story goes that Ragnar was thrown into a pit full of poisonous snakes.

🐞 King Aella was later killed by Ragnar's sons. He is supposed to have been given a truly terrible ritual death called the 'Blood Eagle', in which the shape of an eagle is carved into the victim's back.

🐞 Ragnar's sons also killed the Saxon king, Edmund of East Anglia. They tied him to a tree, shot him with arrows, cut him open and then split his body apart.

🐞 One Arab writer mentioned a horrid Viking habit: they used a bowl to wash in, then spat and blew their noses into it – then they handed it on to the next person, who used the same water.

🐛 If a Viking warrior had a bad stomach wound, he'd be given porridge made with onion and herbs to eat. If the wound smelled of onion and herbs afterwards, it meant that the intestines had been pierced and the warrior would know that he would soon die.

🐛 If Saxon children were sick, they could be made to crawl through a hole in a tree, which was supposed to cure their illness.

# BELIEVE IT OR NOT?

**Saxons accused of a crime plunged their hands into boiling water to test if they were guilty.**

Believe it or not, it's true. It was known as trial by ordeal. If someone was accused of a crime but said they were innocent, they could decide between two 'ordeals': water or iron. In the water ordeal, an accused man would have to plunge his hand into a bowl of boiling water and take out a stone. In the iron ordeal, the accused had to carry a bar of red hot iron in his hand for about three metres. In both cases, the hand was bandaged. After three days the bandage would be taken off: if the wound was healing cleanly, the man was innocent, but if it was festering, he was guilty.

ooh

The Saxons built their houses out of 'wattle and daub'. The wattle was made of woven twigs and sticks, and the daub was animal dung mixed with water and straw.

Saxons were either freemen or slaves. Slaves were the property of their master and couldn't leave unless they were sold to someone else or given their freedom. You might become a slave if you were captured in battle, as punishment for a crime or if you'd become so poor and hungry that making yourself a slave was your only chance of survival. A man was allowed to sell his children into slavery as long as they were seven years old or more!

There's a legend about King Edmund's head: it went missing during his horrible execution, but his friends found it when they called out and the head answered! The various bits of poor King Edmund were buried. When he was dug up years later, the head and body had miraculously joined back together.

# GORY STORY: SAINT OSWALD'S REMAINS

Two Saxon kings – Oswald of Northumbria and Penda of Mercia – fought against each other at the Battle of Maserfield in AD 642. Oswald was defeated, killed and chopped into bits. His head, body and limbs were stuck on poles as trophies in the town of Oswestry (the town's name means 'Oswald's tree'). Oswald was made a saint and his remains were rescued. Dead saints' bodies were prized as holy relics, which were supposed to have miraculous powers, and Saint Oswald's remains were no exception. His head was dug up from where it was buried, put in the coffin of Saint Cuthbert (another Saxon saint) and moved to Durham Cathedral, and one of his arms ended up decorated in silver in another church in Durham. Some Yorkshire monks claimed to have quite a lot of Oswald, including an arm. In fact, everyone wanted a piece of Oswald: various churches and monasteries all over England, and even abroad, said they had bones, limbs or other chunks of him. But if they'd all been telling the truth, Oswald would have had dozens of arms and legs, several heads and a lot more bones than the rest of us!

🐞 Every nine years the Vikings held a massive sacrifice to their gods at Uppsala in Sweden. Nine men were killed, along with nine of any type of animal the Vikings could find. Then the grisly remains of the people and animals were hung from trees in a sacred grove.

🐞 The chief Saxon god, who was called Woden, had one eye and a raven perched on each shoulder. Hideous human sacrifices were made to him.

🐞 A Saxon remedy to stop a wound from bleeding was to take some fresh horse dung, bake it in the oven, make it into a powder and apply it to the wound with a bandage. You probably won't want to try this yourself!

🐞 People used outdoor loos during the Viking period – in York (known as Jorvik in Viking times), the loos were screened-off enclosures around a wooden plank with a hole in it and a pit underneath. During their excavations, archaeologists found a collapsed loo seat in one toilet pit – we can only hope the person using it didn't end up in the toilet pit as well!

🐞 'Berserkers' were a type of Viking warrior known for their fierce and frenzied fighting in battle. They seemed to have superhuman strength and would dress in bear or wolf skins (or maybe not bother with clothes at all), bite their shields, howl, hammer their weapons against their own helmets, and generally go berserk (it's where the expression comes from).

🐞 Burning bees and then rubbing the ash onto a person's scalp was supposed to cure baldness in Saxon times.

🐞 One group of Danish Vikings are said to have feasted on top of piles of their dead enemies after a battle. The heat of their cooking fires made the dead bodies burst open ... which must have put the Vikings off their dinner.

🐞 Viking slaves (known as thralls) were sometimes given insulting names like Fat Legs, Stupid, Ugly and Big Nose.

🐞 Vikings washed their clothes in cow urine.

🐞 A Saxon cure for madness was to take the skin of a porpoise, make a whip from it and beat the mad person with the whip.

# SAXON & VIKING QUIZ

1. What was a Saxon scramasaxe?

a) A long dagger
b) A public toilet
c) A musical instrument

2. Why might Saxon cows be driven through smoke?

a) To cure foot and mouth disease
b) To get rid of fleas
c) To drive out evil

3. How did the Viking Ragnar Hairy-Breeches get his name?

a) His trousers were absolutely filthy.
b) He wore fur trousers.
c) He had especially hairy legs.

4. Which of the following was supposed to soothe sore eyes in Saxon times?

a) Pepper
b) Sheep dung
c) Beer

5. What happened in the Saxon Blotmonath (known as the month of blood)?

a) The Saxons went to war.
b) A huge black pudding was made.
c) Animals were slaughtered.

6. Which of the following was a Saxon cure for warts?

a) Take a piece of meat, rub it on the wart then bury the meat. As the meat rots away, so the wart will also disappear.
b) Grind up some dead ants and mix them with honey. Apply this mixture to the wart with a bandage and leave it on for a week. The wart should then go away.
c) Bake a sheep dropping for three hours, make it into powder and scatter it in your garden while reciting a prayer.

7. What was a Viking blot?

a) A shield decorated with the skin of a Saxon
b) A sacrifice
c) A toilet pit

8. What was the most common form of execution in Saxon times?

a) Hanging
b) Stoning to death
c) Burning

9. A Saxon law said that you could only eat a hen three months after the hen had eaten what?

a) Pig poo
b) Poppy seeds
c) Human blood

10. What did Viking warriors wear on their chests when fighting?

a) A cotton shirt dipped in enemy blood
b) Chain mail (material made from metal links) or a metal breastplate
c) Nothing at all

# The Norman Perilous Past

🐛 Saxon King Harold is famous for being killed at the Battle of Hastings in 1066 when a Norman arrow pierced his eye. We don't know for certain whether this is true – it is possible that he was hacked down by Norman soldiers first and then shot by an arrow. However, it is also possible that he wasn't shot by an arrow at all.

🐛 After King Harold was defeated at the Battle of Hastings, his relatives asked William the Conqueror for his body so that they could bury it. But William refused to hand over the corpse.

🐛 Rollo the Viking was given land by King Charles the Simple of France and became the first Norman. The story goes that he was supposed to kiss Charles's foot, as was the custom, but didn't fancy it. He picked up Charles's foot instead, knocking Charles over backwards.

heh heh

🐞 Earl Waltheof rebelled against the Normans and had his head chopped off as a result. The story goes that he was in the middle of saying a prayer when the executioner swung his axe – the severed head was seen and heard by witnesses to finish the prayer.

🐞 William the Conqueror's dad was known as Robert the Devil! He was given his nickname because he was suspected of killing his own brother.

# BELIEVE IT OR NOT?

**An army of children went to fight in the Crusades.** Believe it or not, it's true. Perhaps as many as 50,000 children from France and Germany set off on a crusade (a religious war) in 1212. They were trying to reach the Holy Land, but most gave up or were sold as slaves before they got there.

🐞 When William the Conqueror died his body was too big for the stone tomb that had been made for him and it had to be forced in. His corpse smelled so bad that the priests had to rush through the funeral service.

🐞 William the Conqueror's tomb was opened twice in the 16th century. Most of the skeleton went missing – only the thigh bone was left, but that was reburied inside a grand monument. In 1792 the monument was demolished and only a stone remains to mark the final resting place of William's thigh.

William Aetheling, Henry I's son and heir, died in a shipwreck in the English Channel. The White Ship Disaster meant that Henry had to find a new heir, which led to another disaster - a big fight between Stephen and Matilda, who both claimed the throne.

William the Conqueror wanted to crush the rebels in the north of England so he destroyed farms, crops and animals, and killed all the men he could find. Their bodies were left to rot and the survivors were left to starve.

Odo, William the Conqueror's half-brother, was made Bishop of Bayeux when he was just 13 years old.

The punishment for a Norman soldier convicted of cowardice was to have his hand pierced with a hot iron.

Henry I died after eating too many eels.

🐞 The unpopular William II (also known as William Rufus) was killed in a hunting accident in 1100. Walter Tirel claimed to have been aiming at a deer but hit the king in the heart instead. People were suspicious … but no one seemed to mind too much.

🐞 William the Conqueror died in terrible pain: his horse stumbled and William's stomach was horribly injured by the saddle.

🐞 King Stephen was Henry I's nephew. He said that he supported his cousin Matilda's claim to the throne of England (she was Henry I's daughter), but he didn't really like the thought of a woman ruler and fought her for the crown.

hands off!

🐞 Matilda came up with a clever escape plan when she was trapped in the Wiltshire town of Devizes by Stephen's soldiers – she pretended to be dead. She must have made a convincing corpse because she got away with it and made her escape.

🐞 William II was buried under the tower of Winchester Cathedral. When the tower fell down a few years later, people blamed the wickedness of William's bones.

🐞A Norman knight's favourite sport was hunting. They used hounds and birds of prey to hunt foxes, deer, hares, badgers, otters and rabbits. Hunters also drove wolves into traps, then beat them to death, and hunted down wild boar with spears.

🐞William the Conqueror is supposed to have screamed with fear on his deathbed because he was terrified of going to hell.

🐞Henry I had his own brother locked up in Cardiff Prison until he died, when he was 80 years old.

🐞Having your eyes put out was a punishment for poaching one of William the Conqueror's deer. You could lose a hand for simply disturbing one of William's animals!

🐞Saxon King Harold fought against Viking Harald Hardrada before he fought William the Conqueror at the Battle of Hastings. Harold beat his Viking enemy: the Viking invasion force arrived in 300 ships but the survivors went home in just 24.

🐞Many Norman knights went off to fight in the Crusades. The Pope said that any of them who died fighting would automatically go to heaven.

🐞In 1084 the Normans were supposed to be defending the city of Rome. Instead they destroyed it, killed loads of people and then left the bodies to rot in the streets.

William's half-brother, Odo, fought his own nephew (William the Conqueror's son) for the throne of England. The fact that Odo was a bishop didn't seem to stop him.

# GORY STORY: HANDS OFF

Before he became King of England, William the Conqueror besieged the town of Alençon in France. William was rumoured to be the grandson of a tanner (a leather worker) so, to make fun of his humble origins, the town's defenders hung animal skins over the walls. William took offence at this and decided to teach the people of Alençon a lesson. He took 34 prisoners, cut off their hands and feet and threw the bits back over the walls of the town. After the revolting rain of hands and feet, Alençon surrendered.

🐞 Women were supposed to be meek and obedient during the Norman period. There's a story that William the Conqueror's wife, Matilda, agreed to marry him even after he beat her!

🐞 When Saxon Hereward the Wake returned to his family house in 1068 he found that William the Conqueror had nicked it and given it to a Norman lord. To make matters even worse, Hereward's brother's head was stuck on a pole above the entrance to the house! Hereward got revenge for his brother's death by killing 15 Norman soldiers and sticking their heads on poles in place of his brother's.

🐞 The New Forest was created so that William the Conqueror and his friends could have somewhere to hunt. All of the villages that got in the way were destroyed to make room for it.

🐞 Some Norman knights were mercenaries - in other words they'd fight for anyone who paid them. Normans fought as mercenaries against foreign invaders in Italy, but they ended up conquering a large chunk of southern Italy themselves!

🐞 Norman leader William Iron Arm earned his nickname when he ferociously charged at the Emir of Syracuse and killed him single-handedly. He soon became the most powerful ruler of southern Italy.

# NORMAN QUIZ

1. What was the Norman Domesday Book?

a) A book of prophesy
b) A record of crimes and their punishments
c) A record of land and property

2. Which of the following was a Norman fashion?

a) Long dresses for men
b) Shoes with long points
c) False 'beauty spots' worn on the face

3. How many kings of England were there in 1066?

a) Two
b) Three
c) Four

4. In 1066 which of the following was seen as a bad omen for King Harold?

a) A strange star was seen in the sky.
b) Harold's horse suddenly dropped dead while he was riding it.
c) He broke his sword the day before the Battle of Hastings.

5. The Normans built simple castles – an earth mound with a ditch around it, a wooden wall on top and an enclosed courtyard below. What's this type of castle called?

a) Wattle and daub
b) Glaive and cuirass
c) Motte and bailey

6. How did Viking Harald Hardrada die at the Battle of Stamford Bridge against King Harold of England?

a) He was shot in the chest by an arrow.
b) He was shot in the eye by an arrow.
c) He was battered to death with a mace.

7. What was the first thing William the Conqueror did when he landed on the south coast of England?

a) He killed a peasant.
b) He fell flat on his face.
c) He stuck his Norman flag in the ground.

8. What was a Norman hauberk?

a) An outside loo
b) A chain mail tunic
c) A rowdy drinking party

9. What were King Harold's housecarls?

a) Slaves
b) Soldiers
c) Wives

10. Which of these was built by William the Conqueror soon after he became King of England?

a) The Tower of London
b) Leeds Castle
c) Westminster Abbey

# The Medieval Perilous Past

🐛 Henry II fell out with his friend Thomas Becket, the Archbishop of Canterbury. When he complained about him, his knights rushed off to Canterbury Cathedral where they hacked Thomas to death.

🐛 Henry II said he hadn't meant for Thomas Becket to be killed. He found some strange ways of apologising: one was to have monks beat him with branches while he walked barefoot through Canterbury, before spending the night in Becket's tomb.

🐛 Edward IV of England executed his own brother for plotting against him. He is supposed to have had him drowned in a barrel of wine.

🐛 During the medieval period one writer recorded that starving people ate all sorts of things such as dogs, cats, bird poo and even their own children.

Richard I of England died after he was shot by a crossbow bolt. The wound became gangrenous – it rotted and eventually killed him.

King John was accused of being a werewolf!

Medieval hairdressers didn't just cut hair – they cut off limbs too. Some of them also had another role as a tooth-puller.

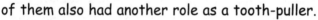

During the Middle Ages John the Baptist's head was supposed to have somehow ended up at Amiens Cathedral in France, where pilgrims visited it in the hope that it would perform a miracle. Another French cathedral also claimed to have John the Baptist's head – they argued over who had the real one!

Even before the Black Death arrived, England had been struck by death and disaster: freezing cold and wet weather led to floods, failed crops and sick animals, all of which resulted in famine.

Handkerchiefs were not common in the Middle Ages (though Richard II is supposed to have invented them). Most people just blew their noses into their fingers.

Henry III set up a zoo in the Tower of London. It was home to three leopards, a polar bear and an elephant.

If you had toothache during the Middle Ages you'd pop down to the local tooth-puller. Some people cleaned their teeth using powder that was made from crushed shells, which wasn't very good for their tooth enamel. Not surprisingly, bad breath was very common ... but then again so was BO.

To avoid scars from the disease smallpox, people used to drink a mixture of sheep droppings and wine. It didn't stop them getting scars but it might well have given them a different disease.

If you were a bit hard of hearing in medieval times, one remedy was to leave a dead eel to rot in horse manure, then stick the rotten eel in your ear.

# GORY STORY: THE BEASTLY BEGINNING OF THE BLACK DEATH

The Black Death was the name given to an outbreak of plague that killed millions of people in Europe between 1347 and 1350. The disease itself was absolutely foul: victims would develop a high temperature, aches and pains, and horrible swellings called buboes. They'd start to vomit, their skin would turn black and after two or three days they'd be dead. There's a gory story about how the Black Death arrived in Europe...

In 1346 the town of Caffa, a port on the Black Sea, was besieged by an army of Tartars from central Asia. Plague broke out among the Tartar troops and thousands fell ill and died. Janibeg, the Tartar commander, was forced to give up and go home, but he couldn't resist giving the besieged town a parting gift: he gave the order for the dead bodies of the plague victims to be loaded into catapults and fired over the city walls. The revolting rain of bodies quickly spread the disease. Merchants returned from Caffa to their homes in Italy and brought the plague with them.

🐛 After Edward I's death, his body was boiled down to the bones so that they could be carried into battle.

🐛 When Henry IV became King of England in 1399, onlookers noticed that his hair was crawling with lice as the crown was put on his head.

🐞 The Black Death was so horrible, and killed so many, that you can see why people turned to desperate measures to try and cure it. None of them worked, though...

**Revolting Cures for the Black Death #1:** Simply strap a live chicken to one of your plague sores and you won't be in a flap

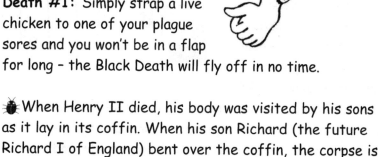

for long – the Black Death will fly off in no time.

🐞 When Henry II died, his body was visited by his sons as it lay in its coffin. When his son Richard (the future Richard I of England) bent over the coffin, the corpse is supposed to have spurted blood over him.

🐞 Instead of toilet paper, medieval people used a scraper called a gompf stick.

🐞 **Revolting Cures for the Black Death #2:** Bend over the nearest toilet pit, or a foul-smelling drain, and take some nice deep breaths. The horrible odour will drive off the disease. Take care not to fall in, though, or the smell will also drive off your friends.

stinky

# BELIEVE IT OR NOT?

**Pigs appeared in court in the Middle Ages.**
Believe it or not, it's true. It seems that medieval pigs were more aggressive creatures than the ones we know today and they were sometimes known to kill

small children. Just like anyone else accused of murder, pigs (and other animals too) were charged with their crime, put on trial and even had a lawyer to defend them in court. For a crime like murder the punishment would be the death penalty, usually by hanging.

🐛 Medieval doctors' favourite remedy was bloodletting – cutting the patient and letting them bleed – which they thought would make most things get better. They didn't seem to notice that it just made things worse.

🐛 More than 20,000 peasants marched on London in order to protest about taxes and low wages during the Peasants' Revolt of 1381. When they arrived in London, they captured and executed the Lord Chancellor (who was also the Archbishop of Canterbury) and the Lord Treasurer.

🐞The leader of the Peasants' Revolt had a meeting with the king at Smithfield in London, where he was dragged from his horse and run through with a sword by the Lord Mayor of London. Other peasant leaders were hunted down, tortured and killed.

🐞Henry IV had a large growth underneath his nose and sores all over his body.

🐞Edward III came to the throne after his father, Edward II, had been murdered on the orders of his mother and her boyfriend (Queen Isabella and Roger Mortimer).

🐞During the medieval period, people simply emptied their chamber pots out of their windows. They would call 'Gardy loo!' to warn passers-by to watch out - it comes from the French words *guardez l'eau*, or 'mind the water', and that's where we get our word 'loo'.

🐛 Wealthy medieval ladies are said to have used goose feathers as loo paper, which must have been quite ticklish.

🐛 The poet Geoffrey Chaucer worked for the king as well as writing poetry. He went to Italy on the king's business and stayed with the Visconti Brothers, a gruesome twosome who were famous for their cruelty and for torturing people. Chaucer was also the victim of crime – he was mugged twice on the same day!

🐛 Edward I was determined to take the crown of Scotland for himself and decided to terrify the Scots by destroying Berwick (a border town that was then in Scotland). He had all the townspeople killed and left the bodies to rot in the streets.

🐛 Carrying a dead shrew in your pocket was a medieval cure for rheumatism.

🐛 Trebuchets and mangonels were huge catapults that were used in sieges during the medieval period. Dead animals, dung and even dead people were all used as missiles.

In 1297 Scottish leader William Wallace defeated the English at the Battle of Stirling Bridge. Wallace is supposed to have stripped the skin off the dead English leader, Hugh Cressingham, and used it as a belt.

William Wallace was executed by being hanged, drawn and quartered. Different bits of his body were sent to towns in England and Scotland as a warning to traitors. His head ended up on a pole on London Bridge.

In the city of Milan in Italy, plague victims were walled up in their homes with the other members of their family, whether they were sick or not, in an attempt to stop the plague from spreading.

Henry V of England died while he was in France. His body was boiled up until only the bones were left, then the skeleton was sent back to England to be buried.

**Revolting Cures for the Black Death #3:** Foul smells drive away the bad air thought to cause the Black Death. Unfortunately, you can't always produce a foul smell when you need one. So, fart into a bottle and cork the bottle quickly. Then the bottle acts as a portable cure for any bad air that you might come across when you're out and about.

🐞 Castles had toilets called garderobes and these emptied into the moat or a toilet pit. People kept their clothes in them because the smell kept moths away.

🐞 A medieval religious group called the Flagellants beat themselves with whips with metal tips, in order to pay for their sins.

🐞 **Revolting Cures for the Black Death #4:** The Black Death is caused by bad blood, so opening a vein should help get rid of it.

🐞 The Countess of Buchan defended Berwick Castle so fiercely against King Edward I of England that, when he finally overcame her soldiers, he hung her over the battlements in an iron cage.

# GORY STORY: THE PRINCES IN THE TOWER

Twelve-year-old Edward V didn't last very long on the throne – his uncle Richard made sure of that. Richard was meant to be Edward's 'Protector', but he didn't do much protecting. Instead he got a bishop to say that Edward's parents had never really been married, so that Edward wasn't allowed to be king. Then Uncle Richard became King Richard III instead of the young boy he was supposed to be looking after.

Richard III threw Edward and his nine-year-old brother into the Tower of London and the two princes were never seen again. No one really knows what happened to them. However, hundreds of years later, workers on a staircase at the Tower of London unearthed two skeletons: they were young boys aged about 12 and 9. The finger of suspicion points at Richard III, who might have had the poor children murdered and then hidden their bodies.

However, Richard III got his comeuppance in the end: he was killed at the Battle of Bosworth in 1485 and Henry Tudor became king. Richard was buried but it is said that his bones were later thrown out and his coffin was used as a horse trough.

Urine was often collected from castles, monasteries or anywhere lots of people lived together. Then the pee was sold to the leather trade and used in the leather-making process.

# MEDIEVAL QUIZ

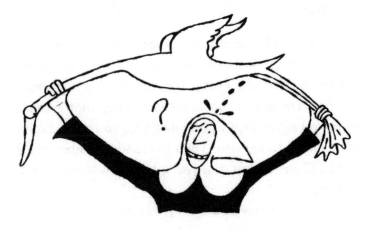

1. What began in 1337 and ended in 1453?

a) The Hundred Years War
b) The plague
c) The reign of Edward II

2. Who was the Black Prince?

a) Edward III's son, who wore black armour
b) Edward II's son, who died of the Black Death
c) Edward I's son, who rode a black warhorse

3. How did King James II of Scotland die in 1460?

a) He was struck by lightning.
b) He was shot through the heart by an arrow.
c) A cannonball shot off his leg and he bled to death.

4. On average, how long did people live in Britain during the Middle Ages?

a) 15 years
b) 30 years
c) 60 years

5. Why might you tie a string of worms around your neck in the Middle Ages?

a) To cure a sore throat
b) To ward off evil spirits
c) As a lucky charm

6. Which of the following was a medieval remedy for a nosebleed?

a) Sniff a chamber pot
b) Burn a mixture of dried dung and duck feathers and inhale the smoke
c) Stick stinging nettles up your nose

7. What happened to Joan of Arc, who led a French army against the English?

a) She was burned at the stake.
b) She was beheaded.
c) She was hanged.

8. Who was Wat Tyler?

a) An outlawed nobleman
b) A ruthless earl
c) A revolting peasant

9. During the Middle Ages, what did people throw at weddings instead of confetti?

a) Dried horse manure
b) Sawdust
c) Tomatoes

10. Why might you slap goose droppings on your head in the Middle Ages?

a) To say sorry for your sins
b) To get rid of head lice
c) To cure baldness

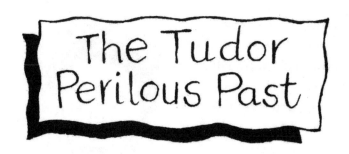

# The Tudor Perilous Past

🐛 Henry Tudor defeated Richard III at the Battle of Bosworth and became the first Tudor king as Henry VII. But there were at least 10 other people with a better claim to the throne of England than Henry.

🐛 At Hampton Court, one of Henry VIII's palaces, servants all shared the same enormous loo. Fourteen people could use it at the same time.

🐛 A Tudor cure for warts was to put half a mouse on the wart, then bury the other half of the mouse in the ground.

🐛 In Tudor times a mixture of hare's brain, goose fat and honey was rubbed into a baby's gums if the baby was teething. The cure sounds worse than aching gums!

🐛 Anne Boleyn, Henry VIII's second wife, supposedly had six fingers on one of her hands.

🐛 Not much was known about dentistry during the Tudor period. Elizabeth I's teeth were completely black and rotten by the end of her life.

🐛 If you wanted some gory entertainment, London was the place to be. You could watch public hangings at Tyburn, beheadings at Tower Hill, burnings at Smithfield, bear-baiting at Bankside and cock-fighting all over town. London Bridge was a popular place for executed criminals' heads to be displayed on poles.

🐛 People who could afford it drank lots of wine and beer. During the Tudor period, water was so dirty that no one drank it unless they had to.

🐛 Mary Tudor only ruled as queen of England for five years before Elizabeth I came to the throne, yet she gave nearly 300 people the dreadful sentence of being burned to death during her reign.

🐛 Elizabeth I executed around 200 people for being Catholic. Other executions included her cousin, Mary Queen of Scots, and one of her favourite courtiers, the Earl of Essex. She put Walter Raleigh and his wife in prison just for getting married to one another.

🪲 To get rid of a headache, a Tudor might press a hangman's rope against his or her head.

🪲 Elizabeth I nearly died of smallpox in 1562. The disease could leave its victims with terrible scars: Lady Mary Sidney, who nursed Queen Liz, was badly scarred and never showed her face in court again.

# BELIEVE IT OR NOT?

**In Tudor times it was someone's job to wipe the royal behind of Henry VIII after he'd been to the loo.** Believe it or not, it's true. The king wasn't expected to do anything for himself – not even that. In fact, wiping the king's bum was a top job (and a bottom job too) and was carried out by a highly paid member of court, known as the Groom of the Stool.

🐛 Mary Queen of Scots was beheaded by a clumsy executioner: his first swing of the axe only cut her and he had to have a few more chops before he got the head completely off. When he held up the head for the crowd to see, he ended up holding just the hair – Mary had been wearing a wig.

🐛 One in every five babies died during its first year in Tudor times.

🐛 Henry VIII held a party after the death of his first wife, Catherine of Aragon.

🐛 In 1579 Queen Elizabeth was considering marriage to the Duke of Anjou. A man called John Stubbs wrote a pamphlet criticising the idea. Elizabeth punished him and the publisher of the pamphlet by having their right hands cut off.

Richard Roose was head chef to the Bishop of Rochester. When the bishop upset him, Roose used a poisonous plant in his cooking to upset the stomachs of the bishop and his dinner guests. Two of the guests died and Roose was caught. Instead of being hanged for murder, Roose was sentenced to be boiled alive!

# GORY STORY: SIR THOMAS MORE'S HEAD

Sir Thomas More was Lord Chancellor of England during Henry VIII's reign, but fell out with the king. This was unwise – he soon found himself having his head chopped off.

Thomas's head was given a good boiling to make it last longer, then it was stuck on a pole on London Bridge. Thomas's daughter, Margaret, slipped the bridge-keeper some cash and he handed over the head. It was a gruesome souvenir of her old dad, but Margaret was glad to have it. In fact she was so fond of it that, instead of burying it, she preserved it in spices and hung on to it until her death, 11 years later. Finally, Margaret and her father's head were buried together.

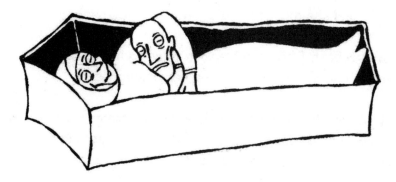

🪲Edward VI, Henry VIII's son, only ruled for six years – he was very sickly and died at the age of 15. He had a very painful death because he was given arsenic in a (misguided) attempt to treat his illness, thought to be a lung disease.

🪲Queen Elizabeth's body was badly embalmed. At her funeral, the body exploded and blew up the coffin.

🪲Having a bath was thought to be unhealthy, so Tudors just covered up the smell of their BO with plenty of perfume.

🪲In the last months of Henry VIII's life, he had to be carried everywhere in a chair because of the seeping sores on his legs. He died a slow and painful death.

🪲Henry VIII's sixth wife, Catherine Parr, was due to marry another man, Thomas Seymour, but couldn't refuse when the king asked her to marry him instead. Catherine nursed Henry during his last years (which must have been pretty foul) but was free to marry Thomas when Henry died, and she did.

🪲Elizabeth I had trouble with thinning hair. She had more than 80 wigs to cover up her balding head.

🪲In the 1500s and 1600s, Egyptian mummies were ground up and used as medicine that was supposed to cure all sorts of different illnesses.

🐞 Rich Tudor people ate some interesting food: stuffed peacocks, swans, larks, beavers, snails and eels, for example. Cooks sometimes served two animals stitched together (a pig and a chicken, for example) or hid live birds inside pastry cases so that they'd fly out and keep the posh guests entertained.

🐞 Drinking milk that a ferret had drunk from was a Tudor cure for whooping cough.

🐞 Lady Jane Grey was 15 when she was put on the throne after Edward VI's death. But after just nine days she was kicked off it again by Henry VIII's daughter, Mary Tudor, and executed a year later.

🐞 Witchcraft was made a crime in Tudor times and hundreds of (mostly) poor old women were accused and found guilty of being witches. The most common punishment for witches in England was hanging.

🐛 The plague wasn't the only disease to be scared of in Tudor times: there were plenty more. One horrible illness known as 'the sweats' delayed Henry VII's coronation because so many people in London had it. If you survived the first couple of days of shivering and sweating and feeling weak, then you might live ... but many people died.

🐛 During the last years of her life, Elizabeth I became convinced that someone was trying to kill her. She would sometimes stab the curtains with a sword in case there was a murderer lurking behind them.

🐛 A courtier was bowing to Elizabeth I when he accidentally farted. He was so embarrassed that he stayed away from court for seven years. When he finally returned, Elizabeth saw him and burst out laughing, saying 'I had forgot the fart!'

🐞 Smoking tobacco became fashionable in Tudor times. When people coughed up disgusting black gunk, they thought it was a *good* thing because they were getting rid of the horrible stuff. They didn't realise they were coughing it up because they were smoking in the first place.

🐞 Being hanged, drawn and quartered was a gruesome punishment in Tudor times: the victim was hanged until almost dead, then was cut open and had his insides burned in front of him, before being beheaded and having his body cut into four pieces.

🐞 William Shakespeare's play *Titus Andronicus* has an absolutely foul plot full of gruesome deaths. At the end two sons are chopped up and secretly served up to their mother in a pie.

🐞 Lady Jane Grey's father, the Duke of Suffolk, was beheaded as a traitor. His head was preserved and put on display until the 20th century, when it was finally buried.

🐞 During the Tudor period, people often used a piece of damp cloth instead of loo roll.

🐞 Artists painting a portrait of Queen Elizabeth I had to follow strict rules so that she always looked the same in paintings and she always looked beautiful.

# GORY STORY: GORDON'S GHASTLY TRIAL

Scottish George Gordon, the Earl of Huntly, led a rebellion against Mary Queen of Scots. His rebellion was defeated at the Battle of Corrichie, in which George was killed, but his story doesn't end there...

Mary Queen of Scots wanted George's land, but she could only get her hands on it if George had been convicted of treason in a law court. He hadn't been, because he was dead, but Mary was very keen on the land and property, plus George had *really* annoyed her. So George's body was carted off to Edinburgh and put on trial for treason. The corpse didn't have very much to say in its defence and was found guilty. It was sentenced to be beheaded and that's what happened. Mary Queen of Scots got her land in the end.

🐞 Tudor sailors desperate for food ate rats, candles and even boiled up the leather from their shoes and ate that.

🐞 Elizabeth I often bashed her ladies-in-waiting when she was in a bad mood.

🐞 Elizabeth I used to make herself vomit with a peacock feather so that she could start dinner all over again.

🐛 In July 1545, Henry VIII watched as his ship, the *Mary Rose*, sank just after leaving Portsmouth Harbour. About 700 men died on board.

🐛 Henry VIII saw a portrait of his fourth wife, Anne of Cleves, before they married and liked what he saw. But when he met her in person he said he thought she looked like a horse and divorced her as quickly as possible. We don't know what Anne thought about Henry's appearance.

# TUDOR QUIZ

1. What was a jakes in Tudor times?

a) A public hanging
b) A toilet
c) A person with bad BO

2. How did Edward VI die?

a) He caught a disease.
b) He was poisoned.
c) He was shot with a musket.

3. What were known as strossers in Tudor times?

a) Underpants
b) Beggars
c) Pickpockets

4. What did Tudors mean by 'plucking a rose'?

a) Burping
b) Having a pee
c) Picking your nose

5. What was strange about Danish astronomer Tycho Brahe?

a) He had the Danish word for thief branded on his forehead.
b) He had false ears.
c) He had a metal nose.

6. Why might a Tudor mother give her baby a horse's tooth?

a) For good luck
b) To keep the Devil away
c) For teething

7. True or false? Tudor children were forbidden from drinking alcohol.

8. What was Henry VIII doing while his second wife, Anne Boleyn, was having her head chopped off?

a) Praying for forgiveness in church
b) On his way to church to marry his third wife
c) Playing tennis

9. What was the usual punishment for a Tudor found guilty of witchcraft?

a) Burning at the stake
b) Hanging
c) Beheading

10. Elizabeth I's godson, John Harington, invented the 'Ajax'. What was it?

a) A flushing toilet
b) An instrument of torture
c) A head-chopping machine

# The Stuart Perilous Past

🐛 In Stuart times bloodletting (cutting open veins and allowing blood to flow) was still the commonest treatment for just about any illness.

🐛 There was a terrible outbreak of plague in England in 1665, known as the Great Plague. The village of Eyam in Derbyshire was almost wiped out by it.

🐛 James I sentenced Walter Raleigh to death in 1603, then decided to let him live. But he didn't tell Raleigh about his change of mind until he was actually on the scaffold about to be executed. (Fifteen years later, Raleigh really was executed on James's orders.)

🐛 A Stuart punishment for drunkenness was to wear a barrel with holes cut in it – called a 'Drunkard's Cloak' – and parade through the streets.

🐛 Rock Braziliano was a pirate during the 1670s. He was famous for his cruelty and is supposed to have roasted two men alive.

🐛 In the 1600s, scientist Santorio Sanctorius spent 30 years weighing all the food and drink he put into his body ... and everything that came out too!

## BELIEVE IT OR NOT?

**Sir Walter Raleigh's wife kept her dead husband's head in a bag.**
Believe it or not, it's true. The famous explorer Walter Raleigh was executed for treason in 1618. Raleigh's body was buried but his wife, Elizabeth Throckmorton, decided to hang on to his head. She kept it by her side in a red leather bag until her death in 1647. Then Raleigh's son, Carew, looked after the head until he died, when he and the head were both buried in Raleigh's tomb.

🐞 Smoking tobacco was recommended as a plague cure during the 1600s.

🐞 Thousands died in the Great Plague of 1665. Carts went around cities collecting dead bodies and taking them to huge mass graves known as plague pits.

🐞 By 1640, tobacco had become so popular that it was London's biggest import. People smoked it in pipes rather than in cigarettes.

🐞 James I once stuffed a live frog down the Earl of Pembroke's tunic. The earl got his revenge by putting a pig in the king's bedroom.

🐞 When someone was beheaded in the 1500s and 1600s, the head would be boiled with salt and spices to preserve it, then displayed on a pole.

🐞 Judge George Jeffreys was nicknamed the Hanging Judge because of his habit of sentencing people to death. During the Bloody Assizes in 1685 (the trial of people accused of plotting to overthrow James II of England as part of the Duke of Monmouth's rebellion), he sentenced 74 people to be hanged in Dorset and 253 people to be hanged, drawn and quartered in Somerset.

🐞 King James I of England was fascinated by witches and wrote a book about them.

🐞 When famous scientist Isaac Newton studied at Cambridge University he had a job emptying chamberpots.

# GORY STORY: THE WITCHFINDER GENERAL

Finding witches was a popular pastime during the 1600s. Matthew Hopkins seemed to have a special talent for it: he was given the title Witchfinder General and went about the countryside tracking down anyone who practised witchcraft. Of course, the people he accused weren't really witches – they were mostly poor old ladies. But that didn't stop Hopkins finding and executing at least 200 of them. Hopkins was highly paid for every witch he discovered, which he did by dunking his suspects in the nearest pond: anyone who floated was guilty and should be put to death; anyone who sank was innocent after all (but dead, unfortunately). The punishment for being a witch was to be put to death.

You'll be pleased to hear that after all this Matthew Hopkins got the fate he so richly deserved: one day, someone accused him of being a witch and an angry crowd hauled him off to a pond to find out whether or not he was guilty. Hopkins floated. We don't know what happened next, but it's likely that the Witchfinder General was executed on the spot by the people who might have been his next victims.

🐞 Sir Arthur Aston, a general in the English Civil War, was defeated by Cromwell's troops in Ireland and beaten to death with his own wooden leg.

🐞 In the 1600s, a chamber pot was known as a 'rogue with one ear'.

🐞 All of Queen Anne's 18 children died young – 17 of them when they were babies and one when he was 11.

🐞 Guy Fawkes, who was caught trying to blow up the Houses of Parliament in 1605, was horribly tortured until he confessed (he could barely sign his name on the confession because he was so weak from his ordeal). A committee was set up to try and think of a really horrible punishment for him, but he ended up being hanged, drawn and quartered because no one could think of a worse one.

# GORY STORY: OLIVER CROMWELL'S HEAD

Oliver Cromwell got rid of the monarchy in England when he chopped off King Charles I's head in 1649. Cromwell became the leader of the English Parliament himself. When he died in 1658 he was given a grand funeral and his body was embalmed and buried in Westminster Abbey.

Two years later, people decided they wanted the monarchy back again and Charles II became king. No one was keen on Oliver Cromwell any more (after all, he'd chopped off the old king's head), so his body was dug up and hanged on a gallows in front of a huge crowd. Then Cromwell's head was cut off and stuck on a pole on the roof of Westminster Hall. It stayed there for 24 years, until it was blown off in a gale. A soldier picked it up and kept it for a while, before passing it on to someone else. Even though Cromwell's head had been embalmed, it couldn't have been very pretty. In 1710 it turned up in a freak show, labelled 'The Monster's Head'.

In 1960, someone took pity on Cromwell's head and it was presented to the college where he'd studied. It was finally given a resting place in the college grounds and hasn't been dug up since.

🐞 After the Bloody Assizes in 1685 the bodies of the executed people were preserved in tar and put on display around the west of England as a warning to anyone thinking of rebelling against the king.

🪲 François L'Ollonais was a 17th-century pirate known for gruesome methods of torture. Eventually he got his just desserts: he was passing through Central America where he was captured by the people who lived there – they killed him, chopped him up and burned the bits.

🪲 At the public execution of Charles I, some members of the crowd came forward to dip pieces of material in the dead king's blood to take away as gruesome souvenirs.

🪲 Charles I's head was sewn back on to his body after he'd been beheaded so that he could be buried whole.

🪲 Samuel Pepys's famous diary records that he kissed the mouth of a queen. However, it was no ordinary queen. He was talking about the preserved corpse of Katherine de Valois, wife of Henry V, which went on display in the 1600s. Katherine had been dead for 200 years.

royal gout

🐞 Queen Anne was a large lady. She also had swollen legs because of a disease called gout. She had to be carried to her own coronation.

🐞 Charles I's wife, Henrietta Maria, died and was buried in France, but during the French Revolution, people who hated the monarchy dug her body up again.

🐞 Children were often encouraged to smoke because people wrongly thought it was good for them. At the famous public school Eton, the pupils were told to smoke to drive off the plague.

🐞 Charles II is supposed to have moved the Royal Observatory to Greenwich after a raven's poo splattered his telescope at the old observatory at the Tower of London.

🐞 When James I was staying at Gowrie Castle in Scotland, before he became King of England, his bodyguards killed two of his friends, thinking that they were trying to kill James. James felt that they should be given a trial, so the dead bodies were taken away to Edinburgh where they were found guilty and hanged.

# BELIEVE IT OR NOT?

**The town of Halifax had its own head-chopping machine.**

Believe it or not, it's true. The town of Halifax in Yorkshire had a head-chopper, a bit like the French guillotine, to execute criminals. There was a slim chance for a condemned prisoner to escape: if the criminal could pull his head out of the machine before the blade came down and sliced it off, he could run for the parish border. If he made it across, he was free. Amazingly, one man managed it but was stupid enough to return to Halifax a few years later. He was condemned to be executed again and this time he didn't get away. The last time the machine was used was in 1648.

The famous scientist Isaac Newton poked sticks into his eye sockets as part of his experiments. He was very lucky that he didn't blind himself.

During the Stuart period, women wore make-up made from powdered pigs' bones so that their faces would look fashionably pale.

🐞 One French visitor to James I reported that the king dribbled when he drank and never washed his hands.

🐞 King William III caught an infection after a horse-riding accident. Doctors tried everything to make him better – including giving him powdered crabs' eyes! Nothing worked and the king died.

🐞 Doctors 'bled' Charles II to try and cure his kidney disease. Not surprisingly, it killed him.

🐞 The town of Colchester in Essex was besieged by Cromwell's Roundheads during the Civil War. The townspeople were forced to eat cats and dogs to survive.

🐞 Just as they had in the Middle Ages, people in Stuart times believed that the plague was caused by bad air. They thought that firing a cannon might get rid of it.

The Duke of Monmouth led a rebellion against King James II (which led to the Bloody Assizes overseen by Judge George Jeffreys) and was beheaded as a traitor. Afterwards, his friends and family realised that the duke had never had an official portrait. So his head was stuck back on his body and the corpse 'sat' for a painter.

The Great Fire of London in 1666 raged for five days and most of the buildings within the city walls were burned to the ground. All sorts of people were blamed for starting the fire, especially foreigners. A French man confessed to starting the fire and was executed for it, even though he couldn't really have been responsible.

# STUART QUIZ

1. What did Queen Mary II die of?

a) Smallpox
b) Measles
c) Flu

2. Which of the following was a Stuart fashion for men?

a) Using duck fat to make their hair stand up in spikes
b) Bleaching their hair with pee
c) Shaving their heads and wearing wigs instead

3. What was a mill-ken in Stuart times?

a) A public toilet
b) A burglar
c) A gallows

4. What did Charles II rub on to his body in the belief that it would make him great?

a) Dust from ancient Egyptian mummies
b) Squashed frogs
c) The powdered bones of Saint Cuthbert

5. Which of these was recommended to clear the lungs and get rid of headaches and indigestion?

a) Breathing in the fumes from a toilet pit
b) Smoking
c) Drinking vinegar mixed with crushed flies

6. Which animals were rounded up and killed by the government because they were thought to spread the plague?

a) Dogs
b) Pigs
c) Rats

7. Which of the following was a cure for spots in Stuart times?

a) Applying fresh horse manure
b) Applying the blood of a freshly killed pigeon
c) Applying fresh morning dew

8. Which of the following did Stuart people believe would keep your teeth white?

a) Brushing with powdered cats' bones
b) Smoking
c) Sleeping with your mouth open

9. Which of the following might you find at a Stuart fair?

a) A snail-eater
b) A toad-eater
c) A beefeater

10. Queen Anne's doctors tried which of the following to cure her gout?

a) Feeding her jellied eels and jugged hare
b) Covering her in lard and pigs' blood
c) Applying hot irons and covering her feet in garlic

# The Georgian Perilous Past

🪲 After Admiral Horatio Nelson died at the Battle of Trafalgar in 1805, his body was pickled in a barrel of spirits until his ship arrived back in England. The story goes that the sailors drank the alcohol after his body was removed.

🪲 Britain traded in slaves from Africa until 1807, when the trade was banned. In the last half of the 1700s, more than two million slaves were shipped to America.

🪲 The English had a reputation for being fat and greedy in Georgian times.

🪲 Georgian daredevil Jack Mytton had a pet bear. At one of his rowdy parties he tried to ride it and the animal bit a chunk out of his leg.

🪲 King George II died after having a fit and falling off the toilet.

 Georgian eccentric Susanna Kennedy, Countess of Eglintoune, kept hundreds of rats as pets, which ran free about the house. The Countess liked to have dinner with the rats and would call them to the dining table by tapping on a panel.

 French King Louis XVI was guillotined in 1793 during the French Revolution. Some of the people watching soaked pieces of cloth in his blood as mementos of the occasion.

 In the 1700s in Edinburgh, a man provided a portable public loo for passers-by: a bucket and a cloak, which he held up to hide the user.

 There were 63,000 casualties at the Battle of Waterloo in 1815 (the British and their friends fighting against the French).

# BELIEVE IT OR NOT?

**A woman was hanged on a gallows but later woke up in her coffin.**

Believe it or not, it's true. Maggie Dickson was hanged in Edinburgh in 1724. As she was taken away in a coffin, friends and relatives heard banging noises from inside. The coffin lid was lifted and Maggie was found to be alive. She lived for another 40 years and became known as Half Hangit Maggie.

Captain Robert Jenkins claimed that his ear had been cut off by the Spanish when his ship was in a Spanish-controlled part of the Caribbean, and in 1738 he showed the ear to the House of Commons. Britain went to war with Spain as a result: it was known as the War of Jenkins' Ear.

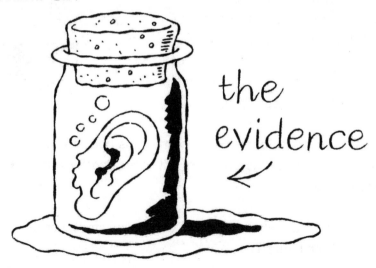

the evidence ←

🐞 John Hunter was a surgeon in Georgian times. Because there weren't many people who were happy to be experimented on after they'd died, he ended up body-snatching fresh corpses from graveyards.

🐞 In 1819 in St Peter's Fields in Manchester, a crowd of thousands of people met in peaceful political protest – they were charged by soldiers and 11 of them were killed. (It became known as the Peterloo Massacre, named after the Battle of Waterloo.)

🐞 Georgian foundation make-up included poisonous lead paint and arsenic powder.

🐞 Edward Teach, better known as Blackbeard, was probably the cruellest and most ruthless pirate of them all. Drinking with his crew one evening, he suddenly fired a shot underneath the table – it hit his first mate in the kneecap and crippled him for life.

🐞 The surgeon John Hunter wanted his body to be used for dissection by his students after his death – and he got his wish.

🐞 George III believed he was dead and wore mourning clothes for himself.

🐛 Blackbeard was killed by British troops in 1718 after five bloodthirsty years as a pirate. His head was cut off and stuck on the prow of a British ship.

## GORY STORY: CAPTAIN COOK'S AWFUL END

After many years of exploring on the high seas, Captain James Cook met with a gruesome end. In 1779 he was visiting Hawaii but had stayed rather too long and a group of Hawaiians attacked and killed him. Cook's crew wanted their captain to be buried at sea and asked the Hawaiians for his body. At first nothing happened, but after a while, disgusting parcels began to arrive at Cook's ship: first came a package containing Captain Cook's thigh, then some burnt bones, a pair of footless legs, two arms, two hands, a skull and a scalp (which had been given a haircut). The horrible bits and pieces were given a sea burial. What happened to the rest of Cook remains a mystery.

🐞During the 1700s, the English legal system became known as the Bloody Code, because so many crimes were punished by death. In 1815 there were 225 crimes that carried the death penalty... **Crazy crimes that carried the death penalty #1:** In Georgian times you could be executed for stealing goods worth more than one shilling.

# BELIEVE IT OR NOT?

**George III's Royal Surgeon used a bit of a dead king as a salt cellar.**

Believe it or not, it's true. Sir Henry Halford was the Royal Surgeon to King George III. In 1813 he examined the skeleton of Charles I, who had been executed in 1649. During the examination, Sir Henry secretly stole one of the bones in Charles's spine. He enjoyed shocking friends at dinner parties by using the bone as a gruesome salt cellar. Queen Victoria found out about this horrible habit 30 years later and she was not amused. She made Sir Henry return the bone to Charles I's skeleton.

🐞Hannah Beswick died in 1758 but her body wasn't buried: her doctor had made her a promise because she was afraid of being buried alive. So he had her corpse embalmed and kept it in a grandfather clock in his house.

 George III suffered from mental illness. As a cure, doctors stuffed his mouth with handkerchiefs so he couldn't answer back, then shouted at him.

 King George IV's dead body, which had expanded and looked as though it was about to explode, only just fitted inside his coffin. Before he was buried, holes had to be drilled into the coffin to allow the trapped gases to escape.

 If a Georgian criminal was lucky enough to find a crime that didn't carry the death penalty, the punishment was still horrible: he or she might be whipped or branded with a hot iron.

 James Lowther, Earl of Lonsdale, had a girlfriend who died young. The earl had her body embalmed and placed it in a glass-topped coffin, which he kept on display in his dining room.

# GORY STORY: BURKE AND HARE

William Hare owned a lodging house in Edinburgh. One of his lodgers died owing money to another lodger, William Burke. So Hare came up with an idea: he'd heard that surgeons needed dead bodies to practise on and would pay money for nice fresh ones - why not sell the dead lodger's body to a surgeon and get Burke his money back? Burke and Hare took the corpse to an Edinburgh surgeon and they were very pleased with the money they received for it – more than enough to pay back the debt.

However, Burke and Hare became greedy. They decided to make money by secretly digging up freshly buried bodies from graveyards to sell to surgeons. Lugging dead bodies around Edinburgh was grisly work, and tiring too, but it was well paid. It wasn't long before Burke and Hare realised there was a demand for more corpses than they could supply. So they took their gruesome trade a step further: they began luring people back to the lodging house and murdering them, then selling their victims to the surgeons.

Eventually Burke and Hare were caught, but not before they'd murdered at least 15 people. Burke was hanged in 1829. Hare had sneakily given evidence against his partner and was allowed to go free. But he ended up miserable as a beggar on the streets of London.

🐛 Edward Low was an especially vicious pirate in the 1700s. He was famous for cutting off people's lips and ears.

🐞 Another Georgian punishment was to be locked in a pillory: this was placed in a public area, where people could come and throw things at you – dung was a popular choice of missile.

🐞 New Georgian machinery meant that textile workers lost their jobs (because one machine could do the work of several men). Some people tried to stop the job losses by smashing the machines. During the worst of the machine-wrecking, some factory owners were murdered and the murderers were hanged. The youngest to be hanged was a boy of 15.

🐞 **Crazy crimes that carried the death penalty #2:** In Georgian times you could be executed for being out at night with a blackened face.

🪲 The poet Percy Bysshe Shelley drowned in 1822. His body was cremated but his heart was saved from the flames and given to his wife, Mary Shelley, who kept it until her death in 1851.

# BELIEVE IT OR NOT?

**You can still see the body of a Georgian criminal and the Irish Giant on display in London.**
Believe it or not, it's true. Jonathan Wild was a famous criminal in Georgian times. When he was finally caught in 1725 he was taken to Tyburn gallows and hanged. His body was dissected by a surgeon and ended up in the Hunterian Museum at the Royal College of Surgeons, London, and his skeleton is still there today.

Charles Byrne was 2.5 metres tall and known as the Irish Giant. The Georgian surgeon John Hunter got his hands on Byrne's corpse once he'd died. He boiled the body to end up with just the skeleton, which is also on display at the Hunterian Museum to this day.

The museum is named after John Hunter. The kidney of Hunter's father-in-law and the bladder of his local vicar are also kept at the museum.

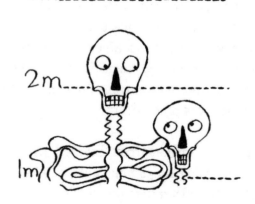

108

🐞Some criminals who didn't get the death penalty might be transported to Australia. More than 130,000 convicts were transported there between 1788 and 1818.

🐞In the 1700s, people were reported to die mysteriously from the 'night air'. Now the 'night air' is explained as poisonous gases that escaped from toilet pits.

🐞George I accused his wife, Sophia, of having a boyfriend. He had her locked her up in the castle of Ahlden, Germany, where she died 32 years later.

🐞**Crazy crimes that carried the death penalty #3:** In the Georgian period you could be executed for stealing from a rabbit warren.

🐞If you saw a pirate ship hoisting a red flag in the 1700s, it meant that the pirates would show no mercy – anyone who got in their way would be killed.

🐞Both men and women wore a lot of heavy make-up in Georgian times. Women wore false eyebrows made from mouse skins.

# GEORGIAN QUIZ

1. What was a slamkin in Georgian times?

a) A woman who was a bit of a slob
b) A man with a personal hygiene problem
c) A child who had fleas

2. Which of the following was ordered by George II?

a) The last ever beheading at the Tower of London
b) The last ever burning at the stake at Smithfield
c) The last ever hanging at Tyburn gallows

3. How many people were hanged in London in 1750?

a) 5
b) 50
c) 500

4. What happened to Prime Minister Spencer Perceval in 1812 that's never happened since?

a) He shot and killed a political rival in the House of Commons.
b) He was assassinated.
c) He attacked the leader of the opposition with a harpoon.

5. Why did George III have a mixture of crushed beetles and mustard applied to his body?

a) To cure his madness
b) To cure his baldness
c) To cure his sore throat

6. Which of the following was a Georgian cure for toothache?

a) Powdered dogs' teeth
b) Crushed spiders
c) Squashed fish eyes

7. What were hippo and walrus tusks used to make in Georgian times?

a) False eyes
b) False teeth
c) False arms and legs

8. Why did Georgian women put cork balls inside their cheeks?

a) To make their breath smell sweet
b) To stop them from feeling hungry
c) To make them look beautiful

9. What did British general Lord Raglan lose in 1815 that Admiral Lord Nelson had lost in 1797?

a) His eye
b) His arm
c) His mind

10. What did Georgian sailors know as bargemen?

a) Maggots that lived in the food rations
b) Sailors who carried out brutal punishments like flogging
c) The ship's toilets

# The Victorian Perilous Past

🐛 Frank Buckland, a Victorian naturalist, was keen to experiment with new foods: he ate elephant's trunk soup, rhinoceros pie, mice cooked in batter, kangaroo, squirrel, giraffe, crocodile and hedgehog. Frank's father, William Buckland, ate the mummified heart of King Louis XIV of France.

🐛 Working people in Victorian towns were often crammed together in cramped housing. They would usually share an outside loo called a privy. As many as 100 people might share the same one.

🐛 If you lived in a city, the disease most likely to kill you was cholera, a perilous disease caused by dirty water that gives sufferers terrible diarrhoea. Just one epidemic, in 1848-1849, killed approximately 60,000 people.

🐛 During the Victorian period, people thought that snail tea would cure a chest infection.

# BELIEVE IT OR NOT?

**London stank so badly in 1858 that the Houses of Parliament had to close.**

Believe it or not, it's true. Victorian London was horribly pongy at the best of times: dead animals, factory waste, horse manure and sewage were all dumped straight into the River Thames. In 1858 there was a hot summer and the whiff became worse – Queen Victoria and her husband, Prince Albert, took a cruise on the Thames but had to turn back because of the smell. Soon no one could go near the river without going green and holding their nose. The Houses of Parliament are right next to the Thames and MPs tried hanging chemical-soaked blankets at the windows to stop the stench, but it didn't work very well. The smelly summer of 1858 became known as the Great Stink.

After the Great Stink of 1858, the government finally had a proper sewer system built. More than 130 kilometres of sewers were built to carry two billion litres of water (and other stuff) every day.

Victorian boys often wore dresses until they were six years old.

Workers in match factories suffered from a horrible disease known as 'phossy jaw' caused by handling the chemical phosphorus. Sufferer's jawbones rotted away and even glowed in the dark.

If you went to an 'unrolling' in the 19th century, you'd see an Egyptian mummy being unwrapped.

A Victorian anatomist called Richard Smith wrote a book about the human body, based on his examination of a hanged criminal's corpse. He even covered the book with the skin of the criminal, which had been made into leather.

Public executions were still a very popular form of entertainment in the Victorian period. Rich people would sometimes hire houses opposite gallows where criminals were hanged so that they could watch in comfort.

🐞 Karl Marx, the 19th-century German writer and thinker, was a bit of a lager lout. He once went on a pub crawl in London and ended up chucking paving stones at street lamps with his drunken mates.

🐞 Prince Albert caught the disease typhoid in 1861, probably from dirty drains at Windsor Castle. He died within a few weeks.

🐞 Poisonous additives in food often led to stomach upsets, or even death. The poison strychnine could be found in beer, and poisonous mercury and lead were found in chocolate.

🐞 Workers in wallpaper factories could be poisoned by the arsenic used in dyes.

# GORY STORY: PICKLED PRINCE HENRY

Prince Henry of Battenberg was married to Princess Beatrice, one of Queen Victoria's daughters. On a trip to West Africa in 1895 he caught the disease malaria and died. Prince Henry's body was loaded on to a ship to be transported back to Britain, but it soon started to rot in the hot weather. Prince Henry's insides were removed in an attempt to stop it from rotting any further, but it didn't seem to help. The ship's crew came up with a clever solution to the problem: they found some biscuit tins and made them into a coffin, put Prince Henry inside and covered his body with rum to preserve it. The body arrived in England pickled and was given a grand funeral on the Isle of Wight.

🐛 Tiny waists were very fashionable in Victorian times. One woman was admired for her 33-centimetre waist but she was later found dead: her corset had been so tight that it injured her insides and killed her.

🐛 Victorian scientist Charles Darwin was described by his teacher as 'entirely dull'.

The Victorians hadn't quite worked out the rules of hygiene. Having a baby in a Victorian hospital was much more dangerous than having one at home.

A tosher was a person who hunted for treasure in Victorian sewers.

# BELIEVE IT OR NOT?

**There were seven attempts to murder Queen Victoria.** Believe it or not, it's true. The first time was in 1840, when she was shot at twice while riding in her carriage, and the last was in 1882. She was lucky enough not to be injured at all during any of the attempts to assassinate her. Each time Victoria's subjects were so full of sympathy that Victoria wrote in a letter, 'It is worth being shot at to see how much one is loved.'

🐞A Victorian remedy for the disease dysentery was to drink powdered human bones mixed with red wine.

🐞Queen Victoria's Scottish servant, John Brown, loved boozing. He invented a ghastly cocktail for Queen Vic – red wine mixed with Scotch whisky!

🐞Prince Christian, the husband of Queen Victoria's daughter Helena, went shooting with his brother-in-law, Arthur. Arthur accidentally shot Christian in the eye and he had to wear a glass eye after that. Christian liked  to show people his collection of eyes – he had a bloodshot one that was his favourite.

🐞After Prince Albert died in 1861, Queen Victoria had servants lay out his clothes every morning just as if he was still alive – this went on for 40 years.

🐞The Anatomy Act was passed in 1832. It allowed dead bodies that weren't claimed by friends or relatives to be given to surgeons for dissection. So body-snatching became less common than in Georgian times.

🐞'Pure Collectors' had the revolting job of collecting dog poo in Victorian towns. They'd sell the poo to tanners, who used it to make leather.

A violet cart didn't smell sweet: it trundled through Victorian streets collecting human waste from toilets.

# GORY STORY: HAVING THE REVEREND FOR DINNER

The Reverend Thomas Baker travelled to the islands of the Pacific trying to spread Christianity. He arrived at a remote village on the island of Viti Levu in Fiji, where he met the chief. In the course of their meeting, the Reverend removed a comb from the chief's head. It was a fatal mistake: touching the chief's head was strictly forbidden. The villagers clubbed Baker and his followers to death, then cooked and ate them!

In 2003, Fijian people from the same village slaughtered a cow and presented woven mats and whales' teeth to descendants of the Reverend Baker, to say sorry for the Reverend's unfortunate end.

🐛 Perforated toilet paper went on sale in Britain for the first time in 1880.

🐛 Queen Victoria didn't like the idea of the lower classes going to school - she thought it stopped them from being good servants!

🐛 Mice in red wine was a remedy for the disease jaundice during Victorian times.

🐛 Victorian Thomas Crapper didn't invent toilet paper or flushing toilets, as many people think, but he did manufacture toilets in the 19th century.

🐛 Queen Victoria's eldest son, Edward (who later became Edward VII), wasn't a good student. According to his teacher, he spat, threw things, swore, pulled faces, threatened his little brother and called his teacher names.

🐛 Until the 1840s, some five-year-old children worked in coal mines opening trapdoors to let coal carts through.

🐛 Many Victorians thought women weren't as clever as men. In 1879 a French scientist even said that a lot of women's brains were closer in size to gorillas' brains than men's!

🐛 Victorian prisons discouraged inmates from talking to one another. They had to wear masks when they were exercising to stop them from recognising each other!

🐛 Workhouses were for poor people who were desperate and had nowhere else to go. They were not designed to be comfortable and conditions were absolutely terrible in many of them. At the workhouse in Andover, Hampshire, in 1845, the people were given the job of breaking up bones – instead they gnawed on them because they were so hungry.

🐛 Mudlarks were poor children who searched for valuables on the shores of the River Thames in London. They had to wade through the raw sewage that emptied straight into the river.

The Victorians thought that showing any flesh – especially a lady's – was absolutely shocking. If they wanted to swim in the sea, many Victorians used bathing machines, which looked a bit like beach huts on wheels, so that no one would see them in their swimming cossies.

Queen Victoria lived to a ripe old age and outlived three of her nine children. After she died, her body was put on display in the dining room at Osborne House, her home on the Isle of Wight. It must have put everyone off their dinner.

During the Victorian period, the poisonous substance mercury was used to make hats. Hatters would end up with the poison in their blood, which could make them go mad. That's where the expression 'as mad as a hatter' comes from.

# BELIEVE IT OR NOT?

**You can find a stuffed philosopher at University College, London.**
Believe it or not, it's true. In 1832 the philosopher Jeremy Bentham died. He had left his body to science and it was dissected by students. Afterwards, the body was stuffed with straw, preserved and displayed at University College, London. It's still there to this day.

# VICTORIAN QUIZ

1. What killed about 140,000 British people between 1831 and 1866?

a) The disease cholera
b) The plague
c) The Crimean War

2. According to French scientist Gustav le Bon, what was as rare as a gorilla with two heads?

a) An honest poor person
b) A useful servant
c) A clever woman

3. What was toilet paper known as in Victorian times?

a) Curl paper
b) Necessary paper
c) Unmentionable paper

4. What were The Waterfall and The Deluge?

a) Two of Thomas Crapper's toilets
b) Victorian bathing machines
c) Two of London's new main sewers

5. Which of the following was a Victorian remedy for earache?

a) Snip some hairs of a cat's tail, mix them with red wine and pour it in your ear.
b) Burn a dead mouse, mix it with honey and stick it in your ear.
c) Hang a dog's tooth around your neck.

6. What was Queen Victoria talking about when she said, 'An ugly [one] is a very nasty object and the prettiest is frightful when undressed'?

a) Servants
b) Babies
c) Men

7. Prince Edward, Queen Victoria's eldest son, once had a part in a play in a London theatre. What was his role?

a) A slave
b) A Roman emperor
c) A dead body

8. If you tried to get a frog to breathe into your mouth, or swallowed a spider covered in butter, what would you be hoping to cure?

a) A cold
b) Whooping cough
c) Measles

9. Queen Victoria's son, Alfred, got a shock at his 25th wedding anniversary celebration in 1899. What happened?

a) Queen Victoria died during the party.
b) His son shot himself during the party.
c) His wife left him during the party.

10. A Victorian London county medical officer found bed bugs, fleas, straw, human hair, and cat and dog hairs in which of the following foods?

a) Ice cream
b) Porridge
c) Bread

# The 20th-Century Perilous Past

🐞 King Edward VII was very fond of food. He would often eat 10-course meals and regularly ate 5 meals a day. In his later years his waist measured more than 1.2 metres!

🐞 Rich Edwardians could be extravagant: dinner for 20 people might cost around £60. In 1910, it took a butler a whole year to earn that much, and *five years* for a scullery maid to do so.

🐞 Until 1908, children who had been convicted of a crime could be sent to an adult prison.

🐞 During the Second World War certain foods, including meat, were rationed – you could only have a small amount of them. Some people were so desperate for a meaty meal that they mixed mashed potatoes, lentils and onions together, shaped them to look like a roast bird and called it Mock Duck.

The Russian Revolution leader, Vladimir Lenin, had his brain removed after he died in 1924. German scientist Oskar Vogt spent over two years studying it and then published a paper reporting that the brain seemed to be especially clever.

In some posh Edwardian homes, the family wouldn't bother learning the names of the more lowly servants – they'd just give them new ones. Footmen were often called James and John, housemaids were often known as Emma.

# GORY STORY: EINSTEIN'S BRAIN

Albert Einstein was the most famous scientist of the 20th century. After he died in 1955, Einstein's body was cremated but his brain was removed. A scientist at Princeton Hospital, Dr Harvey, studied the brain and sliced it into 240 pieces. Dr Harvey gave some pieces of the brain to other researchers, but kept most of it himself in two glass jars. Whenever Dr Harvey moved around the country, he always took Einstein's brain with him. Having kept the brain for more than 40 years, Harvey then gave it to Princeton Hospital in 1996, where it remains to this day. Scientists have decided that one part of Einstein's brain actually is a bit bigger than most people's.

🐛 During the Second World War, British troops had camouflaged toilet paper.

🐛 Glow-in-the-dark false teeth were available in the early part of the 20th century. As well as looking very strange, they were dreadfully dangerous because they were made with the radioactive chemical, radium. You could also buy face creams that contained radium – they were just as dangerous.

🐛 In June 1913, Emily Davison threw herself under the hooves of the king's horse during the Derby horse race. She did it to draw attention to the suffragette movement, which campaigned for votes for women (at the time women weren't allowed to vote in elections). Emily was taken to hospital but died soon afterwards. Five years later, women over 30 won the right to vote and in 1928 women over 21 could vote.

Englishman John Haigh became famous as the Acid Bath Murderer in 1949. He had killed nine people and dissolved their bodies in a vat of sulphuric acid.

In the early 20th century, people were much more easily offended than they are today. Only one actress playing Eliza in George Bernard Shaw's play *Pygmalion* would agree to say the word 'bloody' in the script. When she said it, audiences were shocked.

## BELIEVE IT OR NOT?

**A 20th-century entertainer ate an aircraft.**
Believe it or not, it's true. French entertainer Monsieur Mangetout (Mr Eat Everything) has been eating all sorts of strange things since 1959, including cutlery, televisions, bicycles, shopping trolleys and a *Cessna* light aircraft.

More than 100,000 pigeons served during the First World War and over 200,000 served during the Second World War. They carried messages to and from different parts of the armed forces. The enemy used trained hawks to try to catch the pigeons in order to stop them from delivering their messages. One pigeon, called Mary, received the Dickin Medal – this is the highest award for bravery for animals.

Not all meat was rationed in the Second World War: animals' insides and gristly bits were on sale and there was no restriction on the amount you could eat. So you could eat plenty of hearts, kidneys, brains, intestines, pigs' trotters and sheeps' heads. Truly revolting recipes included brain sauce, and sheep's head and cow-heel stew.

Edward VII was very unhealthy: he smoked 20 cigarettes *and* 12 cigars every day.

In 1944, a spiritualist called Helen Duncan was interrupted during a seance (a sort of ghost-raising meeting) and put in prison under the Witchcraft Act of 1735. It was said that the army was worried she would give away war secrets using her special powers!

🐛 The *Titanic* was a huge ship that was designed to be unsinkable, according to its makers. In 1912 the ship sank on its first ever voyage after hitting an iceberg, killing about 1,500 passengers and crew.

🐛 Today you're allowed to leave some of your school dinner if you don't like it. At some schools in the 20th century, if you left some of your main course and queued up for a pudding, your pudding was plonked on top of what you'd left. So if you left some boiled cabbage, you'd get your semolina slapped on top of it. As a result, lots of schoolchildren ended up with boiled vegetables in their pockets.

🐛 Just after the First World War, there was a worldwide epidemic of flu. Nine million people had been killed in the war; over 20 million were killed by flu.

🐛 In the late 1940s and 1950s, children used Second World War bomb sites as adventure playgrounds. But they were full of sharp, twisted metal, broken glass, buildings that could collapse at any moment and sometimes unexploded bombs. Not surprisingly, plenty of kids were injured and even killed playing on these bomb sites.

🐛 During the Second World War, a London restaurant was fined for serving dead cat, which they said was rabbit.

🐛 Some Edwardian servants would be expected to work from 6 in the morning until 10 or 11 at night. They might get one afternoon off a month as holiday.

🐛 Scientist Marie Curie did brilliant work on radioactivity and discovered the chemical element radium. But she died in 1934 of leukaemia, almost certainly because of her work with radioactive chemicals.

🐛 Harold Davidson was the Rector of Stiffkey in Norfolk but lost his job. In 1937 he joined a fair and preached from a lion's den. One day he trod on the lion's tail – the lion wasn't very pleased so it mauled him and he died a few days later.

🐛 In 1911 Captain Robert Falcon Scott led an expedition to the Antarctic in an attempt to become the first to reach the South Pole. When they got there they discovered that a Norwegian team had beaten them to it. Scott and four of his men died on their freezing journey back from the Pole.

🐛 Fanny Craddock, a celebrity chef from the 1950s, introduced viewers to blue eggs and green potatoes. Everyone was so glad that rationing had ended that they loved them.

🐛 The First World War became known as 'the war to end all wars' (it wasn't, though). In just one battle – the Battle of the Somme in 1916 – 300,000 people were killed and many thousands more were injured.

# GORY STORY: FOUL FORCE-FEEDING

Suffragettes campaigned for women to be allowed to vote in government elections. (Women couldn't vote until 1918 and even then they had to be over 30 years old in order to do so. In 1928 women were finally given the right to vote when they were 21 – the same as men.) They broke the law to draw attention to their campaign and many of them were sent to jail. In prison, one suffragette refused to eat. She was released because the government didn't want her to die and become a suffragette martyr, so lots more women in prison stopped eating. The government didn't want to release them all – otherwise there wouldn't be any point in sending suffragettes to prison in the first place. So the government decided to do something really foul: the women were force-fed through tubes pushed down their throats or up their noses. More than a thousand women were force-fed in prison – some of them died as a result.

🐞 Adolf Hitler, leader of the German Nazi party in the Second World War, was responsible for millions of people's deaths, yet he was a vegetarian and hated to see animals suffer.

🐞 During wartime in the 20th century, dogs, pigs and rats have been used to find landmines, and sea lions and dolphins have been trained to find underwater objects like mines.

🐛 The 'S bend' was a very strange Edwardian fashion (as well as part of a toilet). Special underwear pushed the woman's top half forwards and her bum backwards, making an exaggerated curved shape. Many women had to lean on a parasol for balance.

🐛 In the First and Second World Wars, soldiers would pee in their boots and then leave them over night in order to help soften up the leather.

🐛 Heinrich Himmler was head of the Nazi death squad, the SS. He suggested that the SS officers should wear bells at night, so that any little creatures might hear them and run away without being trodden on.

# BELIEVE IT OR NOT?

**Twentieth-century school children studied the skeleton of their old headmaster.**
Believe it or not, it's true. Romanian headmaster Grigore Alexandru Popescu died in the 1950s and donated his body for educational purposes. For more than 50 years, his school used his skeleton to teach children about the human body.

🐛 Until 1986, teachers could use corporal punishment in most British schools. Caning was a popular punishment – children would be whacked with a long, thin, bendy rod called a cane. Pupils at the famous public school Eton had to bend over a 'flogging block' when they were punished. Private schools have their own punishment rules and some continued to beat children until 1998, when a new law banned them from doing so too.

🐛 British troops weren't given seasickness pills when they were on ships and often there was just one big oil drum for everyone to be sick into.

# 20TH-CENTURY QUIZ

Elvis (the King)

1. What happened to Queen Victoria's granddaughter, Alexandra?

a) She became Tsarina of Russia and was killed during the Russian Revolution.
b) She became Empress of Germany and was killed during the First World War.
c) She became Queen of Spain and was killed during the Spanish Civil War.

2. Professor Gunther von Hagens invented 'plastination' and opened an exhibition based on this technique in 1995. What were the exhibits?

a) Real dead bodies
b) Real animal dung
c) Decomposing dead animals

3. Which of these recipes appeared in a real wartime cook book?

a) Hedgehog Hotpot and Badger Soup
b) Rook Pie and Squirrel Tail Soup
c) Crow Stew and Stuffed Sparrow

4. Who was killed by the famous murderer Dr Crippen in 1910?

a) His receptionist – he strangled her.
b) His patients – he turned off their life-support systems.
c) His wife – he poisoned her.

5. Which of the following alarmed Queen Elizabeth II in 1982?

a) All of her pet corgis were poisoned.
b) She found an intruder in her bedroom at Buckingham Palace.
c) Someone shot at her during the Trooping of the Colour.

6. Famous 20th-century actor Marlon Brando was a big eater. On the set of one of his films in the 1970s, he was reported to have eaten which of the following?

a) Elephant steaks
b) A plate of mixed insects, including locusts, cockroaches and termites
c) A live frog

7. True or false? The King Edward potato was named after King Edward VII.

8. What happened to Simon the cat, rat-catcher of the *HMS Amethyst*?

a) He was court-martialled (put on trial in a military court).
b) He was awarded a medal.
c) He was promoted to Lieutenant.

9. Where did Elvis Presley, the King of Rock and Roll, die in 1977?

a) In quicksand
b) On the toilet
c) In an avalanche

10. The Italian artist Piero Manzoni created canned artwork in the 1960s. What did the cans contain?

a) The artist's own earwax
b) The artist's own hair and nails
c) The artist's own poo

## PREHISTORIC QUIZ

1. c – Examples of Ogham writing have been found in
Britain and Ireland dating from the 300s to the 600s AD.
The prehistoric Celts didn't have their own written
language though – at least not one that we know about.

2. a

3. b – Mistletoe was a holy plant to the Druids and was
used in their religious ceremonies. We kiss under the
mistletoe at Christmas, a tradition supposedly influenced
by the prehistoric use of the plant.

4. c – Dead bodies were often burnt before they were
buried in the prehistoric past.

5. c – One goddess was believed to turn into a crow and
hover over the battlefield, waiting to feast on the dead
warriors. Another appeared on battlefields as a crow with
a rope around its neck.

6. a

7. a – The colour meant something that came from the
Underworld.

8. b – Otzi is the 5,000-year-old mummy that was found in
the Alps.

9. b – The biggest stones at Stonehenge weighed up to

45 tonnes each – and there were no cranes or lorries to help with the work when the monument was built. There weren't even any wheels at that time. So the stones had to be pulled along on wooden sledges placed on rollers that were made from logs.

10. b – Prasutagus's wife was the Celtic warrior queen Boudicca.

# ROMAN QUIZ

1. a

2. c – Epilepsy sufferers were supposed to drink the blood, preferably while it was still warm. There was another belief that eating the livers of dead gladiators would cure the disease too!

3. c – The sauce was made in factories all over the Roman Empire. It was the Roman equivalent of tomato ketchup and a real favourite!

4. a

5. c – The horse, called Incitatus, was going to be given the important title of 'consul'.

6. b – Romulus and Remus were the legendary founders of Rome. The twins were abandoned by their uncle when they were babies, but a female wolf found them and looked after them.

7. b

8. a

9. b

10. True. People had brands (marks made on the skin) removed and we know about a man who had plastic surgery on his earlobes.

# SAXON & VIKING QUIZ

1. a
2. c
3. b
4. a
5. c – Animals that probably wouldn't survive the cold winter were killed as offerings to the Saxon gods.
6. a
7. b – The Vikings made sacrifices at particular times of the year – for example at midwinter (our Christmas time) – and before battles or other important events. Vikings sacrificed animals, but they might also have made human sacrifices to their chief god, Odin.
8. a
9. c – There must have been a lot of hens pecking at pools of people's blood if there was a law made up about it!
10. b

# NORMAN QUIZ

1. c - William the Conqueror ordered the Domesday Book – a record of his kingdom – in 1085.
2. b – Some shoes were so long and pointy that the ends had to be attached the the wearer's knees.
3. b – They were Edward the Confessor, King Harold and William the Conqueror.
4. a – We now think the strange star was Halley's Comet, which can be seen every 75 or so years.
5. c
6. a

7. b – William fell over and got a bloody nose – he said it was a sign that he'd conquer England.

8. b – Hauberks were knee-length tunics and, because they were made of chain mail, they weighed 14 kilograms.

9. b – They were Harold's own troops, a bit like a royal bodyguard.

10. a

# MEDIEVAL QUIZ

1. a – The Hundred Years War lasted 116 years. It was fought between the English and the French, mainly because English kings kept insisting they should be King of France as well.

2. a – The Black Prince was known as a great soldier. He never became king himself because he died a year before his father.

3. c – King James II was killed at the siege of Roxburgh Castle, which was held by the English. But it wasn't an English cannonball that shot off his leg – one of the Scottish cannons exploded.

4. b

5. a – The sore throat would disappear as the worms died.

6. c

7. a – Joan of Arc was just an ordinary young girl, but she ended up leading an army. Long after her gruesome death she was made a saint.

8. c – Wat Tyler led the Peasants' Revolt of 1381.

9. b

10. c

# TUDOR QUIZ

1. b

2. a – Edward caught tuberculosis, a lung disease.

3. a

4. b

5. c – His real nose had been cut off during a sword fight.

6. c

7. False. Children, and adults too, often drank 'small beer', which had very little alcohol in it and was safer than drinking water.

8. c – At least, so the story goes.

9. b

10. a

# STUART QUIZ

1. a

2. c – At least it stopped them from getting head lice.

3. b

4. a – He believed that the greatness of the dead pharaohs would rub off on to him.

5. b

6. a

7. b

8. c

9. b – Toad-eaters appeared to swallow a live toad for the entertainment of fair-goers.

10. c – Gout is a painful illness that makes the joints swell up.

# GEORGIAN QUIZ

1. a
2. a – The last person to be beheaded there was 80-year-old Lord Lovat, who wanted a different king on the throne of England.
3. b – That's nearly one a week – just in one city.
4. b – Perceval was shot dead in the House of Commons – the only British Prime Minister to be assassinated so far.
5. a
6. c
7. b
8. c – The ladies liked the idea of high cheekbones and full cheeks, but it's really hard to imagine how this made them look pretty!
9. b
10. a – Black-headed maggots were often found in ship's biscuit, a dry bread that formed most of the food ration.

# VICTORIAN QUIZ

1. a
2. c
3. a – Victorian women used paper to curl their hair, so they pretended that's how the toilet paper was used. Everyone knew what it was really for though.
4. a
5. b
6. b
7. c – Edward was in the play *Fedora* at the Vaudeville Theatre in London. His girlfriend, Sarah Bernhardt, was

the star of the play.

8. b – Whooping cough is an especially perilous disease that targets young children. It was common in Victorian times.

9. b – Alfred's son was trying to kill himself but didn't aim very well. However, he died two weeks later.

10. a

# 20TH-CENTURY QUIZ

1. a

2. a – 'Plastination', a method of preserving dead bodies, was discovered by the professor.

3. b – The recipes appeared in a book by Marguerite Patten.

4. c

5. b

6. c – He is said to have grabbed the frog from a pond, taken a bite out of it and then thrown it back.

7. True. Edward VII was so fond of food that he had various dishes named after him: a chicken dish, various fish dishes, an apple and the famous King Edward spud.

8. b – Simon is the only cat that has been awarded the Dickin Medal for bravery. It was given to him for his rat-catching skills and because he boosted sailors' spirits even though he'd been wounded.

9. b

10. c